I dedicate this book to people who play Counter-Strike.
And to people who like the show Rick and Morty.

Web Animation using JavaScript

DEVELOP AND DESIGN

Julian Shapiro

PEACHPIT PRESS
WWW.PEACHPIT.COM

Web Animation using JavaScript: Develop and Design

Julian Shapiro

Peachpit Press
www.peachpit.com

To report errors, please send a note to errata@peachpit.com
Peachpit Press is a division of Pearson Education.

Editor: Victor Gavenda
Development editor: Margaret S. Anderson
Project manager: Margaret S. Anderson
Technical editor: Jay Blanchard
Copyeditor: Gretchen Dykstra
Production editor: David Van Ness
Proofreader: Patricia Pane
Compositor: Danielle Foster
Indexer: Jack Lewis
Cover design: Aren Straiger
Interior design: Mimi Heft

ISBN-13: 978-0-134-09666-7
ISBN-10: 0-134-09666-5

9 8 7 6 5 4 3 2 1

Printed and bound in the United States of America

ACKNOWLEDGEMENTS

I would like to thank Yehonatan Daniv for providing support to Velocity's users on GitHub, Anand Sharma for regularly inspiring me with his motion design work, and David DeSandro for writing this book's foreword. I'd also like to thank Mat Vogels, Harrison Shoff, Adam Singer, David Caplan, and Murat Ayfer for reviewing drafts of this book.

CONTENTS

FOREWORD

It's a special time when a developer first discovers jQuery's `.animate()`. I remember trying to animate any part of the page that wasn't bolted to the main content. I created accordions, fly-out menus, hover effects, scroll transitions, magical reveals, and parallax sliders. Turning my websites from cold, static documents into moving, visual experiences felt like I was reaching another level as a web designer. But it was just bells and whistles. I realize now that for all the animation I added, I hadn't actually improved the user experience of my websites.

All the same, it was thrilling. So what makes animation so exciting?

My apartment looks over downtown Brooklyn. I see people walk down the street. Plumes from smokestacks billow up. Pigeons flutter to perch on a ledge. A construction crane raises a section of a building. A single, heart-shaped balloon floats up into the Brooklyn sky (corny, I know, but I literally saw this happen twice). Cars drive over the Williamsburg Bridge. Clouds pass overhead.

The world is in motion.

This is how you expect the universe to work. Things move. Like the movements outside my window, each one is a one-sentence story. Together they tell the larger story of what is happening.

Yet this isn't how digital interfaces work. Those little stories are missing. When things change, you have to fill in the story for yourself. When you press the Next button at an ATM, the screen suddenly changes. Did it move forward successfully? Was there an error? You have to read the screen again to interpret the results of your action. Utilizing motion removes this leap of understanding between interactions. Motion inherently communicates what has changed. It's like writing tiny stories between states.

When a slide transition takes you to the next screen, animation helps you better understand what just happened. Wielding this power is what makes animation so thrilling. Like layout, color, and typography, animation helps you shape and direct the user experience. Animation is more than just making things move. It's designing more effectively, and doing it thoughtfully.

Unfortunately, in the history of web animation, thoughtfulness hasn't always been the highest priority. As developers, we've used Flash, animated GIFs, Java applets, marquee tags, and, more recently, CSS, JavaScript, and SVG to create animation that's been, at best, a level of polish or, at worst, a gimmick. The idea of creating animation that's both high-performance and user-friendly is relatively new.

So it's a good thing you have this book in front of you. Julian Shapiro is one of the principal experts on animation on the web. In creating and supporting Velocity.js, he has developed an intimate knowledge of all the quirks and advantages of using motion on websites. *Web Animation using JavaScript* will give you not only the technical know-how required to implement animation in your websites, but, more importantly, the insights you'll need to use animation effectively and craft compelling user experiences.

Animation libraries and technologies have made motion design more accessible than ever. But not every developer abides by best practices. The past couple of years have seen several trendy anti-patterns come and go. Scroll behavior has been hijacked. Mobile navigation has been pushed into menus accessible only via gestures. While adding animation is within the grasp of anyone who stumbles across `.animate()`, utilizing it to improve the user experience is one of the hallmarks of a dedicated developer. This book will help you become one of them.

> David DeSandro
> February 2015
> Brooklyn, New York
>
> *David DeSandro is the founder of Metafizzy*
> *and author/developer of Masonry and Isotope.*

INTRODUCTION

In the early days of the web, animation was primarily used by novice developers as a last-ditch effort to call attention to important parts of a page. And even if they wanted animation to transcend its niche, it couldn't: browsers (and computers) were simply too slow to deliver smooth web-based animation.

We've come a long way since the days of flashing banner ads, scrolling news tickers, and Flash intro videos. Today, the stunning motion design of iOS and Android dramatically improves the user experience—instead of detracting from it. Developers of the best sites and apps leverage animation to improve the *feel* and *intuitiveness* of their user interfaces. Animation's rise to relevancy isn't just a by-product of improved processing power; it reflects a better appreciation for best practices within the web development community. The tools you use to make a website are now considered less important than the quality of the resulting user experience. As obvious as this seems, it wasn't always the case.

So, what makes animation in particular so useful? Whether it's transitioning between chunks of content, designing intricate loading sequences, or alerting the user what to do next, animation complements text and layout to reinforce your site's intended behavior, personality, and visual sophistication. Does your content bounce into view in a friendly way, or does it whip across the screen? This is the domain of motion design, and the decisions you make will establish the transcendent feeling of your app.

When users recommend your app to others, they'll often try to describe it with words like "sleek" or "polished." What they don't realize is that they're mostly referring to the motion design work that's gone into the interface. This inability of the layman to make the distinction is precisely what great user interface (UI) designers strive for: animations that reinforce the interface's objectives but don't otherwise divert the user's attention.

This book provides you with the foundation necessary to implement animation confidently and in a way that's both technically maintainable and visually impactful. Throughout, it considers the balance between enriching a page with motion design and avoiding unnecessary flourishes.

Why is all of this so important? Why is it worth your time to perfect your transitions and easing combinations? For the same reason that designers spend hours perfecting their font and color combinations: refined products simply feel superior. They leave users whispering to themselves, "Wow, this is cool," right before they turn to a friend and exclaim, "You gotta see this!"

NOTE: If you're unfamiliar with basic CSS properties, you should pick up an introductory HTML and CSS book before reading this one.

CHAPTER 1

Advantages of JavaScript Animation

In this chapter, we compare JavaScript to CSS for the purposes of animation, and introduce the unique features and workflow advantages provided by JavaScript.

In short, we provide the context needed to help you understand everything you'll learn about JavaScript in this book.

JAVASCRIPT VS. CSS ANIMATION

There's a false belief in the web development community that CSS animation is the only performant way to animate on the web. This misconception has led many developers to abandon JavaScript-based animation altogether, forcing them to

- Manage the entirety of user interface (UI) interaction within style sheets, which can quickly become difficult to maintain.
- Sacrifice real-time animation timing control, which is achievable only within JavaScript. (Timing control is necessary for designing animation into UIs that respond to a user's drag input, like those found in mobile apps.)
- Forgo physics-based motion design, which allows elements on a webpage to behave like objects in the real world.
- Lose support for older browser versions, which remain popular throughout the world.

JavaScript-based animation is actually often as fast as CSS-based animation. CSS animation is mistakenly considered to have a significant leg up because it's most often compared to jQuery's animation features, which are in fact very slow. However, alternative JavaScript animation libraries that bypass jQuery entirely deliver fantastic performance by streamlining their interaction with a page.

NOTE: One library of note, which we'll be using throughout this book, is Velocity.js. It's lightweight yet incredibly feature rich, and it mirrors jQuery's animation syntax to help eliminate the learning curve.

Of course, CSS is perfectly suited for hover state animations (turning a link blue when the mouse is positioned over it, for example), which are very often the extent to which basic webpages include animation. CSS transitions fit seamlessly into existing stylesheets, allowing developers to avoid bloating their pages with unnecessary JavaScript libraries. What's more, CSS animation delivers blazing performance out of the box.

But this book will demonstrate why JavaScript is often the superior choice for animations beyond simple hover state animations.

don't conflate JavaScript with jQuery.

GREAT PERFORMANCE

JavaScript and jQuery are falsely conflated. JavaScript animation is fast. jQuery slows it down. Despite jQuery being tremendously powerful, it wasn't designed to be a high-performance animation engine. It has no mechanism to avoid "layout thrashing," in which a browser becomes overtasked with layout processing work while it's in the process of animating.

Further, because jQuery's code base serves many purposes beyond animation, its memory consumption triggers garbage collections within the browser, causing animations to stutter unpredictably. Lastly, due to decisions made by the jQuery team in the noble pursuit of helping novice users avoid sabotaging their UI with bad code, jQuery forgoes the recommended practice of using the `requestAnimationFrame` function, which browsers make available to drastically improve frame rates for web animation.

JavaScript animation libraries that bypass jQuery entirely deliver fantastic performance by streamlining their interaction with a page. One library of note, which we'll be using throughout this book, is Velocity.js. It's lightweight, yet incredibly feature rich, and it mirrors jQuery's animation syntax to help eliminate the learning curve.

This is a topic we'll explore in-depth in Chapter 7, "Animation Performance." By learning the nuances of browser rendering performance, you'll gain a foundation on which to build reliable animations for all browsers and devices, regardless of their individual processing power.

FEATURES

Speed is, of course, not the only reason to use JavaScript—its abundance of features is equally as important. Let's run through a few of the notable animation features that are exclusive to JavaScript.

PAGE SCROLLING

Page scrolling is one of the most popular uses for JavaScript-based animation. A recent trend in web design is to create long webpages that animate new pieces of content into view as the page is scrolled down.

JavaScript animation libraries, such as Velocity, provide simple functions for scrolling elements into view:

```
$element.velocity("scroll", 1000);
```

This scrolls the browser toward the top edge of $element over a duration of 1000ms using Velocity's "scroll" command. Notice that Velocity's syntax is nearly identical to jQuery's $.animate() function, which is covered later in this chapter.

ANIMATION REVERSAL

Animation reversal is a useful shorthand for undoing an element's previous animation. By invoking the reverse command, you're instructing an element to animate back to its values prior to its last animation. A common use for reversal is animating a modal dialogue into view, then hiding it when the user presses to close it.

An unoptimized reversal workflow consists of keeping track of the specific properties that were last animated on each element that may later be subjected to reversal. Unfortunately, keeping track of prior animation states in UI code quickly becomes unwieldy. In contrast, with the reverse command, Velocity remembers everything for you.

Mimicking the syntax of Velocity's scroll command, the reverse command is called by passing "reverse" as Velocity's first argument:

```
// First animation: Animate an element's opacity toward 0
$element.velocity({ opacity: 0 });
// Second animation: Animate back toward the starting opacity value of 1
$element.velocity("reverse");
```

When it comes to JavaScript's animation timing control, there's more than just reversal: JavaScript also allows you to globally slow down or speed up all JavaScript animations currently running. You'll learn more about this powerful feature in Chapter 4, "Animation Workflow."

PHYSICS-BASED MOTION

The utility of physics in motion design reflects the core principle of what makes for a great user experience (UX) on your site: interfaces that flow naturally from the user's input. Put another way, interfaces that pay tribute to how objects move in the real world.

As a simple yet powerful introduction to physics-based motion Velocity offers an easing type based on spring physics. (We'll fully explore the concept of easing in the next chapter.) With typical easing options, you pass in a string corresponding to a pre-defined easing curve (for example, "ease" or "easeInOutSine"). The spring physics easing type, in contrast, accepts a two-item array.

```
// Animate an element's width to "500px" using a spring physics easing of
→ 500 tensions units and 20 friction units
$element.velocity({ width: "500px" }, { easing: [ 500, 20 ] });
```

The first item in the easing array represents the tension of the simulated spring and the second item represents friction. A higher tension value increases the total speed and bounciness of the animation. A lower friction value increases the vibration speed at the tail end of the animation. By tweaking these values, you can give each animation on your page a unique movement profile, which helps to reinforce the differentiation between their individual behaviors.

MAINTAINABLE WORKFLOWS

Designing animation is an experimental process that requires repeated tweaking of timing and easing values to achieve a uniform feel across the page. Inevitably, just when you've perfected your design, a client will request significant changes. In these situations, maintainable code becomes critical.

The JavaScript-based solution to this workflow problem is wonderfully elegant, and it's covered in depth in Chapter 4, "Animation Workflow." For now, here's the short explanation: There are techniques for chaining together individual JavaScript animations—all with differing durations, easings, and so on—such that the timing of one animation does not affect another. This means you can change individual durations without redoing math and you can go back and easily set animations to run either in parallel or consecutively.

WRAPPING UP

When designing animations in CSS, you're inherently limited to the features that the CSS specification provides. In JavaScript, because of the very nature of programming languages, third-party libraries have an infinite amount of logical control over motion design. Animation engines leverage this to provide powerful features that drastically improve workflow and expand the possibilities of interactive motion design. That's what this book is all about: Designing beautiful animations as efficiently as possible.

The next chapter explains how to use this book's JavaScript animation engine of choice: Velocity.js. In mastering Velocity.js, you'll understand how to leverage the features we've just introduced, and many more.

CHAPTER 2

Animating with Velocity.js

In this chapter, you'll learn the features, commands, and options provided by Velocity.js. If you're familiar with jQuery-based animation, you already know how to use Velocity; it functions nearly identically to jQuery's $.animate() function.

But regardless of your existing knowledge, the methodical feature breakdowns in this chapter will introduce you to the nuances of animation engine behavior. Mastering these nuances will help take you from novice to professional. Even if you're already intimately familiar with JavaScript animation and Velocity.js, do yourself a favor and skim this chapter. You're bound to discover something you didn't realize you could do.

TYPES OF JAVASCRIPT ANIMATION LIBRARIES

There are many types of JavaScript animation libraries. Some replicate physics interactions in the browser. Some make WebGL and Canvas animations easier to maintain. Some focus on SVG animation. Some improve UI animation—this last type is the focus of this book.

The two popular UI animation libraries are GSAP (download it at GreenSock.com) and Velocity (download it at VelocityJS.org). You'll work with Velocity throughout this book since it's free under the MIT license (GSAP requires licensing fees depending on a site's business model), plus it boasts incredibly powerful features for writing clean and expressive animation code. It's in use on many popular sites, including Tumblr, Gap, and Scribd.

Oh, and it was created by the author of this book!

INSTALLING JQUERY AND VELOCITY

You can download jQuery from jQuery.com, and Velocity from VelocityJS.org. To use them on your page—as with any JavaScript library—simply include `<script></script>` tags pointing toward the respective libraries before your page's `</body>` tag. If you're linking to pre-hosted versions of the libraries (as opposed to local copies on your computer), your code might look like this:

```html
<html>
   <head>My Page</head>
   <body>
      My content.
      <script src="//code.jquery.com/jquery-2.1.1.min.js"></script>
      <script src="//cdn.jsdelivr.net/velocity/1.1.0/velocity.min.js">
      → </script>
   </body>
</html>
```

When using jQuery and Velocity together, include jQuery before Velocity. That's it! Now you're ready to roll.

USING VELOCITY: BASICS

To get oriented to Velocity, we'll start with the basic components: arguments, properties, values, and chaining. Since jQuery is so ubiquitous, it is also important to look at the relationship between Velocity and jQuery.

VELOCITY AND JQUERY

Velocity functions independently of jQuery, but the two can be used in combination. It's often preferable to do so to benefit from jQuery's chaining capabilities: When you've preselected an element using jQuery, you can extend it with a call to .velocity() to animate it:

```
// Assign a variable to a jQuery element object
var $div = $("div");
// Animate the element using Velocity
$div.velocity({ opacity: 0 });
This syntax is identical to jQuery's own animate function:
$div.animate({ opacity: 0 });
```

All the examples in this book use Velocity in combination with jQuery, and therefore follow this syntax.

ARGUMENTS

Velocity accepts multiple arguments. Its first argument is an object that maps CSS properties to their desired final values. The properties and their accepted value types correspond directly to those used in CSS (if you're unfamiliar with basic CSS properties, pick up an introductory HTML and CSS book before reading this one):

```
// Animate an element to a width of "500px" and to an opacity of 1.
$element.velocity({ width: "500px", opacity: 1 });
```

TIP: In JavaScript, if you're providing a property value that contains letters (instead of only integers), put the value in quotes.

You can pass in an object specifying animation options as a second argument:

```
$element.velocity({ width: "500px", opacity: 1 },
→ { duration: 400, easing: "swing" });
```

There's also a shorthand argument syntax: Instead of passing in an options object as a second argument, you can use comma-separated argument syntax. This entails listing values for duration (which accepts an integer value), easing (a string value), and complete (a function value) in any comma-separated order. (You'll learn what all of these options do momentarily.)

```
// Animate with a duration of 1000ms (and implicitly use the default easing
→ value of "swing")
$element.velocity({ top: 50 }, 1000);
// Animate with a duration of 1000ms and an easing of "ease-in-out"
$element.velocity({ top: 50 }, 1000, "ease-in-out");
// Animate with an easing of "ease-out" (and implicitly use the default
→ duration value of 400ms)
$element.velocity({ top: 50 }, "ease-out");
// Animate with a duration of 1000ms and a callback function to be
→ triggered upon animation completion
$element.velocity({ top: 50 }, 1000, function() { alert("Complete.") });
```

This shorthand syntax is a quick way of passing in animation options when you only need to specify the basic options (duration, easing, and complete). If you pass in an animation option other than these three, you must switch all options to the object syntax. Hence, if you want to specify a delay option, change the following syntax:

```
$element.velocity({ top: 50 }, 1000, "ease-in-out");
```

to this syntax:

```
// Re-specify the animation options used above, but include a delay value
→ of 500ms
$element.velocity({ top: 50 }, { duration: 1000, easing: "ease-in-out",
→ delay: 500 });
```

You can't do this:

```
// Incorrect: Divides animation options between the comma-separated syntax
→ and the object syntax
$element.velocity({ top: 50 }, 1000, { easing: "ease-in-out",
→ delay: 500 });
```

PROPERTIES

There are two differences between CSS-based and JavaScript-based property animation.

First, unlike in CSS, Velocity accepts only a single numeric value per CSS property. So, you can pass in:

```
$element.velocity({ padding: 10 });
```

or

```
$element.velocity({ paddingLeft: 10, paddingRight: 10 });
```

But you can't pass in:

```
// Incorrect: The CSS property is being passed more than one numeric value.
$element.velocity({ padding: "10 10 10 10" });
```

If you do want to animate all four padding values (top, right, bottom, and left), list them out as separate properties:

```
// Correct
$element.velocity({
    paddingTop: 10,
    paddingRight: 10,
    paddingBottom: 10,
    paddingLeft: 10
});
```

Other common CSS properties that can take multiple numeric values include margin, transform, text-shadow, and box-shadow.

Breaking up compound properties into their sub-properties for the purposes of animation gives you increased control over easing values. In CSS, you can specify only one property-wide easing type when animating multiple sub-properties within the parent padding property, for example. In JavaScript, you can specify independent easing values for each sub-property—the advantages of this will become apparent during the discussion of CSS `transform` property animation later in this chapter.

Listing out independent sub-properties can also make your animation code easier to read and easier to maintain.

The second difference between CSS-based and JavaScript-based property animation is that JavaScript properties drop the dashes between words and all words past the first must be capitalized. For example, `padding-left` becomes `paddingLeft`, and `background-color` becomes `backgroundColor`. Further note that JavaScript property names should not be in quotes:

```
// Correct
$element.velocity({ paddingLeft: 10 });
// Incorrect: Uses a dash and doesn't capitalize
$element.velocity({ padding-left: 10 });
// Incorrect: Uses quotes around the JavaScript-formatted property name
$element.velocity({ "paddingLeft": 10 });
```

VALUES

Velocity supports the px, em, rem, %, deg, vw, and vh units. If you don't provide a unit type with a numeric value, an appropriate one is automatically assigned based on the CSS property type. For most properties, px is the default unit, but a property that expects a rotation angle, such as `rotateZ` for example, would be automatically assigned the deg (degree) unit:

```
$element.velocity({
    top: 50, // Defaults to the px unit type
    left: "50%", // We manually specify the % unit type
    rotateZ: 25 // Defaults to the deg unit type
});
```

Explicitly declaring unit types for all property values increases your code's legibility by making the contrast between the px unit and its alternatives more obvious when quickly eyeballing your code.

Another advantage of Velocity over CSS is that it supports four value operators that can be optionally prefixed to a property value: +, -, *, and /. These directly correspond to their math operators in JavaScript. You can combine these value operators with an equals sign (=) to perform relative math operations. Refer to the inline code comments for examples:

```
$element.velocity({
    top: "50px", // No operator. Animate toward 50 as expected.
    left: "-50", // Negative operator. Animate toward -50 as expected.
    width: "+=5rem", // Convert the current width value into its rem
    → equivalent and add 5 more units.
    height: "-10rem", // Convert the current height value into its rem
    → equivalent and subtract 10 units.
    paddingLeft: "*=2" // Double the current paddingLeft value.
    paddingRight: "/=2" // Divide the current paddingLeft value into two.
});
```

Velocity's shorthand features, such as value operators, retain animation logic entirely within the animation engine. This not only keeps the code more concise by eliminating manual value calculation, but also improves performance by telling Velocity more about how you plan to animate your elements. The more logic that is performed within Velocity, the better Velocity can optimize your code for higher frame rates.

CHAINING

When multiple Velocity calls are chained back-to-back on an element (or a series of elements), they automatically queue onto one another. This means that each animation begins once the preceding animation has completed:

```
$element
    // Animate the width and height properties
    .velocity({ width: "100px", height: "100px" })
    // When width and height are done animating, animate the top property
    .velocity({ top: "50px" });
```

USING VELOCITY: OPTIONS

To round out this introduction to Velocity, let's run through the most commonly used options: duration, easing, begin and complete, loop, delay, and display.

DURATION

You can specify the duration option, which dictates how long an animation call takes to complete, in milliseconds (1/1000th of a second) or as one of three shorthand durations: "slow" (equivalent to 600ms), "normal" (400ms), or "fast" (200ms). When specifying a duration value in milliseconds, provide an integer value without any unit type:

```
// Animate with a duration of 1000ms (1 second)
$element.velocity({ opacity: 1 }, { duration: 1000 });
```

   or

```
$element.velocity({ opacity: 1}, { duration: "slow" });
```

The advantage to using the named shorthand durations is that they express the tempo of an animation (is it slow or is it fast?) when you're reviewing your code. If you use these shorthands exclusively, they'll also naturally lead to more uniform motion design across your site, since all of your animations will fall into one of three speed categories instead of each being passed an arbitrary value.

EASING

Easings are the mathematical functions that define how fast or slow animations occur in different parts of an animation's total duration. For example, an easing type of "ease-in-out" indicates that the animation should gradually accelerate (ease in) during the first part then gradually decelerate (ease out) during the final part. In contrast, an easing type of "ease-in" produces an animation that accelerates up to a target speed during the first part of an animation but thereafter remains at a constant speed until the animation completes. An easing type of "ease-out" is the converse of this: the animation starts and continues at a constant speed before it gradually decelerates during the final part of the animation.

Much like the physics-based motion discussed in Chapter 1, "Advantages of JavaScript Animation," easings give you the power to inject personality into your animations. Take, for example, how robotic an animation that uses the *linear* easing feels. (A linear easing produces an animation that starts, runs, and ends at the same velocity.) The robotic feel is the result of an association with linear robotic motion in the real world: Self-guided mechanical objects typically move in straight lines and operate at constant speeds because there's neither an aesthetic nor an organic reason for them to do otherwise.

In contrast, living things—whether it's the human body or trees blowing in the wind—never move at constant speed in the real world. Friction and other external forces cause them to move at varying speeds.

Great motion designers pay homage to organic motion because it gives the impression that the interface is responding fluidly to the user's interaction. In mobile apps, for example, you expect a menu to quickly accelerate away from your fingers when you swipe it off-screen. If the menu were to instead move away from your fingers at a constant speed—like a robotic arm—you'd feel as if the swipe merely set off a chain of motion events that were outside your control.

You'll learn more about the power of easing types in Chapter 3, "Motion Design Theory." For now, let's run through all of Velocity's available easing values:

- jQuery UI's *trigonometric easings*. For a complete listing of these easing equations, as well as interactive demonstrations of their acceleration profiles, refer to the demos on easings.net.

  ```
  $element.velocity({ width: "100px" }, "easeInOutSine");
  ```

- *CSS's easings*: "ease-in", "ease-out", "ease-in-out", and "ease" (a subtler version of "ease-in-out").

  ```
  $element.velocity({ width: "100px" }, "ease-in-out");
  ```

- CSS's *Bézier curves*: The Bézier curve easing allows complete control over the structure of an easing's acceleration curve. A Bézier curve is defined by specifying the height of four equidistant points on a chart, which Velocity accepts in the format of a four-item array of decimal values. Visit cubic-bezier.com for an interactive guide to creating Bézier curves.

  ```
  $element.velocity({ width: "100px" }, [ 0.17, 0.67, 0.83, 0.67 ]);
  ```

- *Spring physics*: This easing type mimics the bouncy behavior of a spring that's been stretched then suddenly released. As with the classical physics equation that defines the motion of a spring, this easing type lets you pass in a two-item array in the form of [tension, friction]. A higher tension (default: 500) increases total speed and bounciness. A lower friction (default: 20) increases ending vibration speed.

```
$element.velocity({ width: "100px" }, [ 250, 15 ]);
```

- `"spring"` *easing* is a predefined implementation of the spring physics easing that's handy to use when you don't want to experiment with tension and friction values.

```
$element.velocity({ width: "100px" }, "spring");
```

Remember that you can also pass in the easing option as an explicitly defined property in an options object argument:

```
$element.velocity({ width: 50 }, { easing: "spring" });
```

Do not be overwhelmed by the number of easing options available to you. You'll most often rely on the CSS easing types and the "spring" easing, which suit the vast majority of animation use cases. The most complex easing type, the Bézier curve, is most often employed by developers who have a highly specific easing style in mind and aren't afraid to get their hands dirty.

> **NOTE:** The rest of the Velocity options in this section must be explicitly passed into an options object. Unlike those already described, these additional options cannot be supplied to Velocity in the shorthand comma-separated syntax.

BEGIN AND COMPLETE

The begin and complete options allow you to specify functions to be triggered at certain points in an animation: Pass the begin option a function to be called prior to the start of an animation. Conversely, pass the complete option a function to be called at the completion of an animation.

With both options, the function is called once per animation call, even if multiple elements are being animated at once:

```
var $divs = $("div");
$divs.velocity(
   { opacity: 0 },
   // Open an alert box right before the animation begins
   {
begin: function () { console.log("Begin!"); },
      // Open an alert box once the animation completes
      complete: function () { console.log("Complete!"); }
   }
   );
```

CALLBACK FUNCTIONS

These options are commonly referred to as "callback functions" (or "callbacks") since they are "called" when certain events occur in the future. Callbacks are useful for firing events that are dependent on the visibility of elements. For example, if an element starts at invisible then animates toward an opacity of 1, it may be appropriate to subsequently trigger a UI event that modifies the new content once users are able to see it.

Remember that you don't need to use callbacks to queue animations onto one another; animations automatically fire sequentially when more than one is assigned to a single element or set of elements. Callbacks are for the queuing of non-animation logic.

LOOP

Set the loop option to an integer to specify the number of times an animation should alternate between the values in the call's property map and the element's values prior to the call:

```
$element.velocity({ height: "10em" }, { loop: 2 });
```

If the element's original height was *5em*, its height would alternate between *5em* and *10em* twice.

If the begin or complete options are used with a looped call, they are triggered once each—at the very beginning and end of the total loop sequence, respectively; they are not retriggered for each loop alternation.

Instead of passing in an integer, you can also pass in true to trigger infinite looping:

```
$element.velocity({ height: "10em" }, { loop: true });
```

Infinite loops ignore the complete callback since they don't naturally end. They can, however, be manually stopped via Velocity's stop command:

```
$element.velocity("stop");
```

Non-infinite loops are useful for animation sequences that would otherwise require the repetition of chained animation code. For example, if you were to bounce an element up and down twice (perhaps to alert the user of a new message awaiting them), the non-optimized code would look like this:

```
$element
    // Assume translateY starts at "0px"
    .velocity({ translateY: "100px" })
    .velocity({ translateY: "0px" })
    .velocity({ translateY: "100px" })
    .velocity({ translateY: "0px" });
```

The more compact and easier to maintain version of this code would look like this:

```
// Repeat (loop) this animation twice
$element.velocity({ translateY: "100px" }, { loop: 2 });
```

With this optimized version, if you have a change of heart about how much the top value should be changed by (currently "100px"), you need only change the top value in one part of the code. If there are many such instances of repetition in your code, it quickly becomes obvious how much looping benefits your workflow.

Infinite looping is tremendously helpful for loading indicators, which typically animate indefinitely until data has finished loading.

First, make the loading element appear to pulsate by infinitely looping its opacity from visible to invisible:

```
// Assume opacity starts at 1 (fully visible)
$element.velocity({ opacity: 0 }, { loop: true });
```

Later, once the data has finished loading, you can stop the animation, then hide the element:

```
$element
    // First stop the infinite loop...
    .velocity("stop")
    // ... so you can give the element a new animation,
    // in which you can animate it back to invisibility
    .velocity({ opacity: 0 });
```

DELAY

Specify the delay option in milliseconds to insert a pause before an animation begins. The delay option's purpose is to retain an animation's timing logic entirely within Velocity—as opposed to relying on jQuery's $.delay() function to change when a Velocity animation starts:

```
// Wait 100ms before animating opacity toward 0
$element.velocity({ opacity: 0 }, { delay: 100 });
```

You can set the delay option with the loop option to create a pause between loop alternations:

```
// Loop four times, waiting 100ms between each loop
$element.velocity({ height: "+=50px" }, { loop: 4, delay: 100 });
```

DISPLAY AND VISIBILITY

Velocity's display and visibility options correspond directly to their CSS counterparts, and accept the same values, including: "none", "inline", "inline-block", "block", "flex", and so on. In addition, Velocity allows for a value of "auto", which instructs Velocity to set the display property to the element's default value. (For reference, anchors and spans default to "inline", whereas divs and most other elements default to "block".) Velocity's visibility option, like its CSS counterpart, accepts the "hidden", "visible", and "collapse" values.

Within Velocity, when the display option is set to "none" (or when visibility is set to "hidden"), the element's CSS property is set accordingly once the animation has completed. This effectively works to hide an element upon completion of an animation, and is useful in conjunction with animating an element's opacity down to 0 (where the intention is to fade an element off the page):

```
// Fade an element to opacity:0 then remove it from the page's flow
$element.velocity({ opacity: 0 }, { display: "none" });
```

> **NOTE:** The code above effectively replaces the jQuery equivalent:
> ```
> $element
>     .animate({ opacity: 0 })
>     .hide();
> ```

QUICK REVIEW OF VISIBILITY AND DISPLAY

For reference, the CSS display property dictates how an element affects the positioning of the elements surrounding it and contained within it. In contrast, the CSS visibility property exclusively affects whether an element can be seen. If an element is set to "visibility: hidden", it will continue to take up space on the page, but its space will simply be represented by an empty gap—no part of the element will be seen. If an element is instead set to "display: none", the element will be fully removed from the page's flow, and all elements within and around it will fill into the removed element's space as if the element never existed.

Note that, instead of removing an element from the page's flow, you can simply mark the element as both invisible and non-interactive by setting its visibility to "hidden". This is useful for when you want a hidden element to continue taking up space on the page:

```
// Fade an element to opacity:0 then make it non-interactive
$element.velocity({ opacity: 0 }, { visibility: "hidden" });
```

Now, let's consider animations in the opposite direction (showing elements instead of hiding elements): When display or visibility is set to a value other than "none" or "hidden", the value is set *before* the animation begins so the element is visible throughout the duration of the ensuing animation. In other words, you're undoing the hiding that occurred when the element was previously removed from view.

Below, display is set to "block" before the element begins fading in:

```
$element.velocity({ opacity: 1 }, { display: "block" });
```

This effectively replaces the jQuery equivalent:

```
$element
    .show()
    .animate({ opacity: 0 });
```

TIP: For a complete overview of Velocity's animation options, consult the documentation at VelocityJS.org.

CONTAINING ANIMATION LOGIC

As with Velocity's delay option, Velocity's incorporation of CSS display and visibility setting allows for animation logic to be fully contained within Velocity. In production code, whenever an element is faded into or out of view, it's almost always accompanied by a change in display or visibility. Leveraging Velocity shorthands like these helps you keep your code clean and maintainable, since it's less dependent on external jQuery functions and free of repetitive helper functions that commonly bloat animation logic.

Note that Velocity includes shorthands for the opacity toggling animations demonstrated above. They function identically to jQuery's fadeIn and fadeOut functions. You simply pass the corresponding command into Velocity as the first argument, and you pass in an options object, if desired, as normal:

```
$element.velocity("fadeIn", { duration: 1000 });
$element.velocity("fadeOut", { duration: 1000 });
```

USING VELOCITY: ADDITIONAL FEATURES

Additional Velocity.js features that are worthy of note include: the reverse command, scrolling, colors, and transforms (translation, rotate, and scale).

REVERSE COMMAND

To animate an element back to the values prior to its last Velocity call, pass in "reverse" as Velocity's first argument. The reverse command behaves identically to a standard Velocity call; it can take options and is queued up with other chained Velocity calls.

Reverse defaults to the options (duration, easing, etc.) used in the element's prior Velocity call. However, you can override these options by passing in a new options object:

```
// Animate back to the original values using the prior Velocity call's
→ options
$element.velocity("reverse");
```

or

```
// Do the same as above, but replace the prior call's duration with a
→ value of 2000ms
$element.velocity("reverse", { duration: 2000 });
```

NOTE: The previous call's begin and complete options are ignored by the reverse command; reverse never re-calls callback functions.

SCROLLING

To scroll the browser to the top edge of an element, pass in "scroll" as Velocity's first argument. The scroll command behaves identically to a standard Velocity call; it can take options and is queued up with other chained Velocity calls:

```
$element
    .velocity("scroll", { duration: 1000, easing: "spring" })
    .velocity({ opacity: 1 });
```

This scrolls the browser to the top edge of the element using a 1000ms duration and a "spring" easing. Then, once the element has scrolled into view, it fades in fully.

To scroll toward an element inside a parent element with scrollbars, you can use the container option, which accepts either a jQuery object or a raw element. Note that the container element of the CSS position property must be set to either relative, absolute, or fixed—static won't do the trick:

```
// Scroll $element into view of $("#container")
$element.velocity("scroll", { container: $("#container") });
```

In both cases—whether scrolling is relative to the browser window or to a parent element—the scroll command is always called on the element *that's being scrolled into view*.

By default, scrolling occurs on the y-axis. Pass in the axis: "x" option to scroll horizontally instead of vertically:

```
// Scroll the browser to the *left* edge of the targeted div.
$element.velocity("scroll", { axis: "x" });
```

Finally, the scroll command also uniquely takes an offset option, specified in pixels, which offsets the target scroll position:

```
// Scroll to a position 50px *above* the element's top edge.
$element.velocity("scroll", { duration: 1000, offset: "-50px" });
// Scroll to a position 250px *beyond* the element's top edge.
$element.velocity("scroll", { duration: 1000, offset: "250px" });
```

COLORS

Velocity supports color animation for these CSS properties: color, backgroundColor, borderColor, and outlineColor. In Velocity, color properties accept only hex strings as inputs, for example, #000000 (black) or #e2e2e2 (light gray). For more granular color control, you can animate the individual red, green, and blue components of a color property, as well as the alpha component. Red, green, and blue range in value from 0 to 255, and alpha (which is equivalent to opacity) ranges from 0 to 1.

Refer to the inline comments below for examples:

```
$element.velocity({
    // Animate backgroundColor to the hex value for black
    backgroundColor: "#000000",
    // Simultaneously animate the alpha (opacity) of the background to 50%
    backgroundColorAlpha: 0.5,
    // Also animate the red component of the element's text color to half
    → its total value
    colorRed: 125
});
```

TRANSFORMS

The CSS transform property performs translation, scale, and rotation manipulations to elements in both 2D and 3D space. It consists of several subcomponents, of which Velocity supports the following:

- translateX: Move an element along the x-axis.
- translateY: Move an element along the y-axis.
- rotateZ: Rotate an element along the z-axis (effectively clockwise or counter-clockwise on a 2D surface).
- rotateX: Rotate an element along the x-axis (effectively toward or away from the user in 3D space).
- rotateY: Rotate an element along the y-axis (effectively leftward or rightward in 3D space).
- scaleX: Multiply the width dimension of an element.
- scaleY: Multiply the height dimension of an element.

In Velocity, you animate these components as individual properties within a property object:

```
$element.velocity({
    translateZ: "200px",
    rotateZ: "45deg"
});
```

USING VELOCITY: WITHOUT JQUERY (INTERMEDIATE)

If you're an intermediate developer who prefers to work in JavaScript without the aid of jQuery, you'll be happy to know that Velocity also works when jQuery is not present on the page. Accordingly, instead of chaining an animation call onto a jQuery element object—as shown in the previous examples in this chapter—the targeted element(s) are passed directly into the animation call as the first argument:

```
Velocity(element, { opacity: 0.5 }, 1000); // Velocity
```

Velocity retains the same syntax as jQuery's `$.animate()` even when it's used without jQuery; the difference is that all arguments are shifted one position to the right to make room for passing in the targeted elements in the first position. Further, the global *Velocity* object is used to invoke animations instead of specific jQuery element objects.

When you're using Velocity without jQuery, you're no longer animating jQuery element objects, but rather raw Document Object Model (DOM) elements. Raw DOM elements can be retrieved using the following functions:

- `document.getElementByID()`: Retrieve an element by its ID attribute.
- `document.getElementsByTagName()`: Retrieve all elements with a particular tag name (e.g. a, div, p).
- `document.getElementsByClassName()`: Retrieve all elements with a particular CSS class.
- `document.querySelectorAll()`: This function works nearly identically to jQuery's selector engine.

Let's further explore `document.querySelectorAll()` since it will probably be your weapon of choice when selecting elements without the aid of jQuery. (It's a performant function that's widely supported across browsers.) As with jQuery's element selector syntax, you simply pass querySelectorAll a CSS selector (the same selectors you use in your stylesheets for targeting elements), and it will return all matched elements in the form of an array:

```
document.querySelectorAll("body"); // Get the body element
document.querySelectorAll(".squares"); // Get all elements with the
→ "square" class
document.querySelectorAll("div"); // Get all divs
document.querySelectorAll("#main"); // Get the element with an id of "main"
document.querySelectorAll("#main div"); // Get all divs within "main"
```

If you assign the result of one of these lookups to a variable, you can then reuse that variable to animate the targeted element(s):

```
// Get all div elements
var divs = document.querySelectorAll("div");
// Animate all the divs
Velocity(divs, { opacity: 0 }, 1000);
```

Since you're no longer extending jQuery element objects, you may be wondering how to chain animations back-to-back, like this:

```
// These chain onto one another
$element
    .velocity({ opacity: 0.5 }, 1000)
    .velocity({ opacity: 1 }, 1000);
```

To reenact this pattern without the aid of jQuery, simply call animations one after another:

```
// Animations on the same element automatically chain onto one another.
Velocity(element, { opacity: 0 }, 1000);
Velocity(element, { opacity: 1 }, 1000);
```

WRAPPING UP

Now that you're armed with an understanding of the benefits of using JavaScript for web animation, plus a grasp of the basics of Velocity, you're ready to explore the fascinating theoretical foundation that underlies professional motion design.

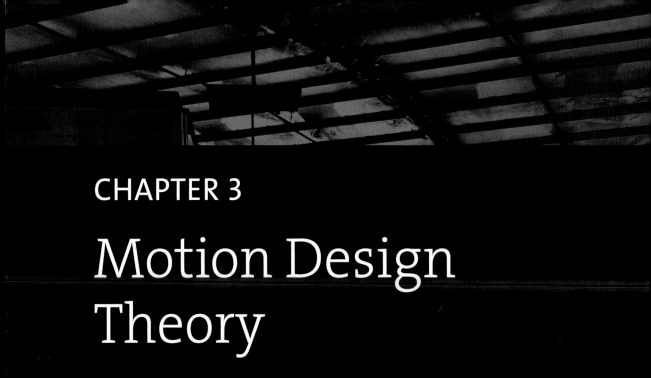

CHAPTER 3

Motion Design Theory

Utility and elegance are the goals of every great motion designer, and this chapter explores a handful of techniques for achieving those goals. Because the focus here is on the theory of motion design—not its implementation—there are no code examples. The techniques discussed can be broadly abstracted across all languages, devices, and platforms.

MOTION DESIGN IMPROVES
THE USER EXPERIENCE

Let's examine the phrase *motion design*: To design *motion* is to decide which visual properties of an object should change, and how that change should accelerate. For example, say you want to call attention to a button by changing its color: you might change the background color from red to blue over a 1000ms duration with an easing style of ease-in-out. In this case, background-color is the target property and red is the desired end value. The timing of the property's transition toward its end value is subject to a 1000ms duration whose acceleration curve is defined by ease-in-out. Great motion designers deliberately choose each one of these components—not because they look good or hit on popular trends, but because they reinforce the intentions of a UI. Whimsical motion design, in contrast, is not only inconsistent, but also appears inelegant and diverting to the user.

There are hundreds of tutorials on the minutiae of UI design, but very few on *motion* design. This isn't surprising given that motion design is less important to a webpage than UI design. Until recently, browsers and devices weren't actually fast enough to accommodate rich motion design. But while UI design lays the structural foundation for interacting with a page, motion design enriches that foundation with the furnishing and decoration that make the page usable and comfortable. Furnishing is the *utility* that motion design serves, and decoration is the *elegance* it provides.

Great apps leverage utility and elegance to make the user feel like she's interacting with an interface that's living, breathing, and tangible. An interface that reacts the way things do in the real world is one that she'll engage with more deeply. In contrast, an interface that's devoid of motion design reminds the user that she's simply dragging a cursor across a screen or tapping her finger on a piece of glass. A UI *without* motion design makes the user painfully aware of the artifice before her.

utility
or
elegance
or
die.

The *utility* of motion design leverages user psychology. When a user presses a button, can she be confident that the press was acknowledged by the UI? An easy way to ensure her confidence is to animate the button's transition to a depressed state. When a user is waiting for content to load, can she be confident that progress is being made or is she left with the unsettling feeling that the app has frozen? These are psychological expectations that motion design can address by providing ongoing visual indications of the UI's state.

The complementary *elegance* of motion design is what elevates an app from merely *looking* good to *feeling* good. It's the source of that "ooh ahh" feeling that reminds the user how magical technology can be.

Let's master both of these aspects. Let's dive in.

UTILITY

How do you ensure your motion design choices are valuable additions to your site? Here are some techniques.

BORROW CONVENTIONS

Let yourself be inspired by the motion design in your favorite sites and apps. Popular motion design conventions are worth leveraging because they already hold meaning in the user's mind. Repeated exposure to conventions leads the user to form *expectations* about how certain animations "should" look. If you use a convention for a purpose other than what the user has come to expect, your app will feel unintuitive.

The more you copy motion design effects from elsewhere, the more familiar your app will feel to the user. The more familiar an app feels, the quicker the user will feel comfortable with it and confident about it. While there's utility in novelty, the motion design of *everyday UI elements* shouldn't be novel. Reserve novelty for animation sequences that carry little meaning or are hard to misconstrue, such as a page's loading sequence or a status indicator animation, respectively.

PREVIEW OUTCOMES

When an element on your page has an ambiguous purpose, give the user a preview of the outcome of interaction. This provides reassurance that the element does what the user thinks it does. A simple example of this would be a button that initiates a file transfer sending out visual radio wave pulses when hovered over. This leverages a common graphic design trope to tell the user that a *data transfer* action will occur.

A less ambiguous kind of previewing outcomes is to show part of the animation that occurs when the user actually takes an action. For example, if an in-progress file transfer indicator animation begins running when the user clicks a button, implement motion design such that hovering over the triggering element *partially* runs the in-progress animation. When the user hovers off the element, reverse the partial animation so the file transfer indicator returns to its default state. This type of previewing technique helps the user immediately understand the effect that her actions will trigger, which helps to reassure her of the purpose of UI elements. The more confident the user feels, the more in control she feels. The more in control she feels, the more pleasant her experience.

DISTRACTION OVER BOREDOM

When a user performs a rote, non-engaging task on your page—such as filling out a long form—you can use color and movement to raise her level of awareness and intrigue. For example, you might animate a check mark when she successfully completes each form field. This keeps the user's mind superficially engaged with the interface, which lessens the dullness of the task at hand. Similarly, you could show the user an eye-catching loading indicator while she waits for content to load. A great example of this can be found in Lyft, a popular ride-sharing app, which animates a balloon rhythmically floating up and down on a blank canvas while the app loads into memory.

Allowing the user's brain to relax and feel the pleasurable momentum of repeated movement keeps her more engaged with your content. However superficial this may seem, it works. But recognize that this technique should be used only in situations where the user will experience an unavoidable stretch of boredom; avoid using it as a Band-Aid any time you feel like spicing up your UI.

Let's consider another example: when Facebook loads text content into its News Feed, it animates a continual blurring of dummy text until the real text is ready to be shown. This rhythmic blurring animation not only indicates that the interface is hard at work (as opposed to having stalled), but also specifically tells the user which portion of the UI she's waiting on. This technique is called *inline status indication*. Compare this to the ubiquitous single status indicator, which is as old as the web itself: the superimposition of a single, looped animation graphic on a page that's discomfortingly devoid of content. Users are tired of this. Inline status indication, in contrast, lets you show *as much of the interface as possible* by blocking out only the specific subsections whose content has yet to load. This is not only more nuanced, but also gives the user more content to fix her eyes on while she twiddles her thumbs waiting for the page to fully load.

The takeaway here is simple: the more you give users to engage with, the longer it'll take for them to get bored.

LEVERAGE PRIMAL INSTINCTS

The human brain has a region dedicated to visual processing. We're programmed to respond to sudden movements whether we want to or not. So, if an important action is occurring on the page that requires the user's immediate attention, consider leveraging movement to flag her attention. A common way to alert the user is to "bounce" an element by repeatedly translating it up and down. This implementation sits in contrast to animating the element's color, which doesn't exploit primal instincts; we're not programmed to instinctively interpret color changes as worthy of our immediate attention. (However, consider how through repeated exposure in some countries, people are trained to interpret red as "stop" and green as "go", which are examples of socially reinforced meaning. When designing motion, take this phenomenon into consideration as well.)

Diving a bit deeper into psychology, the user interprets movement *toward* her as an urgent notice that requires action, whereas she interprets movement *away* from her as getting out of her way and, consequently, not requiring action.

MAKE INTERACTIONS VISCERAL

Big, squishy buttons with rich color gradients make the user want to click. Elements like these reward clicking with a satisfying sense of pressure exertion and color explosion. The lesson here is one of incentivization: the more intriguing it is to click a button, the more a user will do it. Leverage this phenomenon for important calls to action that you want the user to engage with, such as buttons for registering a new account or checking out of a shopping cart.

REFLECT GRAVITAS

If the user has taken an action with irreversible consequences, reinforce that notion by using motion design that feels equally important. For example, the animation associated with clicking a Delete button should feel more significant than the animation associated with hovering over a standard navigation dropdown. While the latter may entail a simple color change, the former might consist of a sudden jump in size and a thickening of the element's border. By divvying up motion design along a gradient of severity, you'll help the user intuitively grasp the hierarchy of the available actions. This technique, along with the others detailed in this chapter, serves the goal of increasing user understanding and confidence.

REDUCE CONCURRENCY

To some extent, users are always trying to make sense of your UI. Consciously or subconsciously, they ascribe meaning to every design and motion design choice you make. So, if you present the user with extended animation sequences consisting of many elements animating into view concurrently, you'll compromise her ability to parse the meaning of all the movements taking place.

In short, if you're using motion design to indicate something important, make sure you're not indicating many different things at once. If you are, consider breaking animations into steps or reducing the total animation count.

REDUCE VARIETY

Related to the best practice of reducing concurrency is the concept of limiting animation variety: the fewer animation variations you have, the more reassured the user will feel that she's fully abreast of what each animation in your UI connotes. For example, if you use one type of animation for bringing big images into view, but a different type for bringing small images into view, consider consolidating them into one. If the differentiation between them was merely for aesthetic purposes rather than for improving usability, you've successfully eliminated unnecessary complexity from your UI, and reinforced behavioral consistency in the process. Consistency leads to pattern recognition and understanding. Understanding leads to increased user confidence.

MIRROR ANIMATIONS

A tangential aspect of limiting animation variety is consistency in your choice of animation property and option combinations. For example, if you have a modal that animates into view by transitioning `opacity` and `scale`, ensure that the modal animates out of view with these two properties reverting to their original values. Don't change properties for the two sides of the same coin. Doing so will make the user question what prompted the differentiation, and needlessly raised questions are the hallmark of a bad user experience.

When working with properties that affect translation (for example, `translateX`, `left`, `marginLeft` in CSS), mirroring applies *literally*: if a modal animates into view by sliding down from the top of the page, have it animate out of view by sliding back up toward the top of the page. Conversely, if you were to have the modal animate out of view by further sliding down off the page, you'd be indicating to the user that the modal has been sent somewhere *new* as opposed to having gone back where it came from. Typically, you want to imply that the modal dialog has gone back where it came from now that the user is done, say, changing account settings. If the user were instead sending an email, then having the modal animate down off the page would be contextually appropriate because it reinforces the idea that the email is being sent from its origin (the user) to a *new* location (the recipient).

LIMIT DURATIONS

Designers often make the mistake of letting animations run too long, causing the user to wait needlessly. Never let UI flourishes slow down the apparent speed of your page. If you have a lot of content fading into view within a larger animation sequence, ensure that the *total* duration across the entire sequence is short.

Similarly, if there's a part of your UI—a profile image, for instance—that transitions into or out of view on a frequent basis due to the way users interact with your page, be extra careful not to allow protracted durations. Seeing a piece of motion design unfold is nice the first time, but seeing it unfold a dozen times every time a user interacts with an app becomes burdensome very quickly—especially if the user feels that repeatedly waiting for the animation to play out is significantly increasing the overall UI wait time.

Since it's difficult to judge the appropriateness of your animation durations after seeing them play out dozens of times during testing, a good rule of thumb is to speed up all animations by 25 percent before you push a site live to production. This will help ensure that they always lean toward the faster side. (See Chapter 4, "Animation Workflow" for tips on how to quickly time-shift your animations.)

LIMIT ANIMATIONS

If removing an animation altogether doesn't detract from the user's understanding of your interface, consider dropping it and using an instant styling change in its place. The more animation you have throughout your UI, the more the user will get used to seeing them. The more she gets used to seeing them, the less attention she'll pay to them, and the less likely she'll be able to differentiate between the different types of motion design and what each signifies.

The vast majority of your motion design should be subtle—minor color changes on hovers, for example—so the few instances of grandiose motion design that do exist should pop to convey their intended message.

don't
be
frivolous.

ELEGANCE

The line between *frivolous* and *consequential* motion design is an easy one to discern: does a particular piece of motion design satisfy one of the best practices discussed in the "Utility" section of this chapter? If not, remove it. It's frivolous, and it's jeopardizing the usability of your UI.

DON'T BE FRIVOLOUS

To hone your judgment about what is frivolous, download the most popular apps, play with each extensively, and judge whether they feature animation to a greater or lesser extent than your app does. Play close to attention to what each animation conveys, and why it conveys it. If you feel that these apps use animation to a much lesser extent than yours does, consider toning back the motion design in your UI.

There's one exception to this don't-be-frivolous mantra—read on!

YOUR ONE OPPORTUNITY TO BE FRIVOLOUS

A page's loading sequence—when all of your elements animate into view from an initial state of invisibility—is your one opportunity to be over-the-top and frivolous with your animations. Why? Because this sequence happens only once, and it won't repeatedly get in the way of the user's interaction with your site. Also, this is your moment to leverage your motion design skills to deliver a great first impression on your site.

If you have a really cool idea for animating your content into view, then do it here. But be sure to respect all the other rules in this chapter, especially **limiting durations**.

CONSIDER PERSONALITY

If you were designing a corporate site, you wouldn't use a bounce effect to transition elements into view. Bounciness is playful—not a quality that corporate sites often want to convey. And if you were designing an educational or government app, you wouldn't use easings that result in movement that starts very quickly before finishing very slowly (thereby conveying a whizzing-by-your-face futuristic slickness)—these would probably be too glossy and stylized for the content at hand.

Always be considerate of the personality expressed by your animation decisions. As a designer, it's hard to judge the tone of your own work, so it's a good idea to get third-party feedback early and often. Ask test users whether a UI feels suitably *professional*, *friendly*, and *sleek*, and tweak your motion design according to your preference for each of those three traits.

GO BEYOND OPACITY

The most common means of transitioning an element into or out of view is to animate its opacity from 0 to 1, and vice versa. This can be rather boring. Opacity is just the base property that has to be animated when displaying or hiding content—it's not the *only* property. You can spice up your property choices by scaling an element down into view, sliding it up out of view, or changing its background color. As you add more properties to an animation, consider leveraging multistep effects, which you'll learn about in the next technique.

BREAK ANIMATIONS INTO STEPS

The simplest path to professional-looking motion design is to break animations into multistep effects. For example, if you're animating an image into view by transitioning its opacity and scale from 0 to 1, instead consider *first* animating the element's opacity to 0.5—half of its final value—followed by animating its scale from 0 while simultaneously animating the remaining half of opacity. Breaking the animations of properties into steps like this removes the linearity that's common to most amateur motion design on the web—wherein all properties animate perfectly in sync. In the real world, the properties of objects in motion don't all accelerate in sync: Consider how, when a bird flies, it moves forward (translateX) at a different rate than it moves up and down (translateY). If it were instead to move linearly in both of its X and Y axes, it would look more like a bullet than an animal. Great motion design borrows from the movement of living, breathing things because UIs are made for humans—not machines—and humans like to feel expression and reaction.

If you pay attention to the futuristic UI animation depicted in movies, you'll notice that intricate multistep animations are a key component in making them look so sleek. The reason for this is simple, and it further supports the case for avoiding linearity: humans are attracted to variety and contrast. Consider how, when you break up an animation, you're contrasting and juxtaposing the individual components of that animation against each other. Just like layering up clothing to create pleasant color and texture combinations, you should layer animations to create pleasant motion design combinations.

For advice on the technical implementation of multistep effects, read Chapter 4, "Animation Workflow."

STAGGER ANIMATIONS

When multiple sibling elements—say, a series of images in a gallery—are animating into view at the same time, consider adding a tiny successive delay between them. (That is, after the first image loads, a delay occurs before the second image loads, and so on.) To delay the animation of sibling elements in this way is called *staggering*, and its purpose is similar to that of breaking an animation into steps: it adds visual layering by preventing all your elements from animating perfectly in sync, which can look plain and inelegant compared to staggered loading. Why? Because animating a series of elements in sync lacks any semblance of granularity or gradience. Consider this: Birds don't fly side by side in a straight line. What makes their aerial movements so graceful is their successive formation and timing. It's their juxtaposition, and the motion of their juxtaposition, that makes them so elegant to the human eye.

FLOW FROM THE TRIGGERING ELEMENT

If clicking a button causes a modal to appear, have the modal animate out from the button's location. In other words, have animations flow from the elements that trigger them. This bridges the cause-and-effect relationships in your UI, making individual elements feel better coupled and better organized.

To understand the psychological benefit of this technique, consider how motion works in the real world: when you pull a lever, a series of mechanical parts causes a *connected* object to move. Connected is the key word: real objects don't move unless a force is exerted upon them. Likewise, it's important to treat every element in your UI as an element capable of exerting its own force. Every action should feel connected to a trigger. This sort of seamless experience is what helps an interface transcend from the digital into the physical. The more physical an interface is, the more responsive and emotive it feels.

USE GRAPHICS

Make use of *scalable vector graphics (SVG)* to animate individual graphic components of a larger element that the user can interact with (learn more in Chapter 6, "Scalable Vector Graphics Primer"). A common example of this is the trio of horizontal lines that constitute a "hamburger menu" icon, or the dots that form a circle in a loading indicator. In both of these examples, arbitrary shapes are grouped together to form a common UI component. Before SVG animation was possible on the web, the common approach to animating a graphic like either of the two described was to embed the full graphic as a PNG image and then animate the entire shape by transitioning its opacity in CSS. By leveraging SVG, however, you can animate these unique elements on an individual shape-by-shape basis and subject them to many types of property animations.

Graphic animation is a surefire way to add nuance to key portions of your UI. This nuance is partially a result of the fact that web-based animation primarily deals with solid, rectangular shapes. (Sometimes they have rounded corners, but the shapes nonetheless remain solid and whole.) Animating the individual shapes of an element instead lets you delight the user with motion design that she might not have realized was even possible.

Beyond novelty, you can also uniquely leverage SVG animation to transform shapes into brand-new ones. Pairing this with the techniques for **previewing outcomes** and **flowing from the triggering element**, you can use graphic transformations to indicate UI behavior and provide feedback to the user. For example, if hovering over the dots in a loading indicator causes those dots to rearrange themselves into an *X* shape, that would indicate to the user that clicking the status indicator graphic would cancel the loading of content.

experiment repeatedly.

EXPERIMENT REPEATEDLY

Finding the right duration, stagger, easing, and property combinations for each animation is *not* a skill that designers are born with. It's a skill that every great designer has had to learn. So, remember: your first attempt at a combination of animation properties might look good, but it's probably not the best case. There are only two ways to find the best case: experiment by systematically changing each factor in the motion design equation until you stumble onto something sublime, or borrow ideas from other peoples' work. Once you've found a combination you like—even if it's one you've already borrowed elsewhere pixel-for-pixel—experiment *further*. Consider cutting the duration in half, switching to a completely different easing type, or swapping out a property.

Designers are often averse to extended experimentation because—even though there are a million ways to animate a button into view—each way effectively fulfills the goal at hand: making the button visible. Consequently, once you stumble onto a combination of properties that look good, you're likely to stick with it because it looks good and it works. But don't forget that goodness isn't a respectable design goal—greatness is. Greatness entails stepping outside your comfort zone, and not necessarily relying on what you already know works.

WRAPPING UP

Utility and elegance are your goals. At minimum, all animation code must fulfill one or the other.

When implemented properly, animation code should provide concrete value to your UX and not adversely impact the website's performance. No matter how sleek your motion design is, if the interface is laggy as a result of its implementation, the overall user experience *will not be elegant*. You'll learn more about the importance of performance in the Chapter 7, "Animation Performance."

CHAPTER 4

Animation
Workflow

The animation code found on most sites is nothing short of a mess. If there's one thing experienced motion designers miss about the old, ugly days of Flash, it's a structured approach to motion design.

The contemporary approach to structuring animation code is twofold: leverage the workflow features of an animation engine (in this case, Velocity.js) to make your code more terse and expressive, and use code organization best practices so that it's easy to modify your work later.

Say goodbye to deep-nesting JavaScript callbacks and to dirtying your stylesheets with unwieldy CSS animations. It's time to up your web animation game.

CSS ANIMATION WORKFLOW

In an attempt to better manage UI animation workflow, developers sometimes switch from JavaScript to CSS. Unfortunately, once animations reach a medium level of complexity, CSS animations typically result in a significantly *worse* workflow.

ISSUES WITH CSS

While CSS transitions are convenient when used sparingly in a stylesheet, they're unmanageable in complex animations sequences (for example, when all elements sequentially load into view upon page load).

CSS tries to address this issue with a keyframes feature, which lets you separate animation logic into discrete time ranges:

```
@keyframes myAnimation {
    0% { opacity: 0; transform: scale(0, 0); }
    25% { opacity: 1; transform: scale(1, 1); }
    50% { transform: translate(100px, 0); }
    100% { transform: translate(100px, 100px); }
}
#box { animation: myAnimation 2.75s; }
```

This specifies separate points within an animation's timeline at which particular property values should be reached. It then assigns the animation to an element with an ID of #box, and specifies the duration of the keyframe sequence to complete within. Don't worry if you don't fully grasp the syntax above—you won't be using it in this book. But before moving on, consider this: what happens when a client asks you to make the opacity animation one second longer, but keep the rest of the properties animating at their current durations? Fulfilling this request requires redoing the math so the percentage values properly align with a 1-second increase. Doing this isn't trivial, and it certainly isn't manageable at scale.

WHEN CSS MAKES SENSE

It's important to point out a situation in which you *should* be using CSS rather than JavaScript for UI animation: when you're animating simple style changes triggered by a user hovering over an element. CSS transitions lend themselves beautifully to these types of micro-interactions, allowing you to accomplish the task in just a few lines of very maintainable code.

Working in CSS, you first define a `transition` on the target element so that changes in the specified CSS properties animate over a predetermined duration:

```
/* When this div's color property is modified, animate its change over
→ a duration of 200ms */
div {
   transition: color 200ms:
}
```

You then specify the value that each particular CSS property should change toward, per the `transition` rule. In the case of the hover example, the div's text color will change to blue when the user hovers over it:

```
div:hover {
   color: blue;
}
```

That's it. In only a few lines of code, CSS handles interaction state for you: when the user hovers away from the div, CSS will animate the change from blue back to the preexisting text color over a duration of 200ms.

WHAT DOES GOOD CODE LOOK LIKE?

Good code is *expressive*, meaning that its purpose is easy to grasp. This is crucial not only for coworkers attempting to integrate your foreign code, but also for yourself in the future, once you've forgotten your original approach. Good code is also *terse*, meaning that it accomplishes what it needs to in as few lines as possible; every line serves an important purpose, and it can't be rewritten away. Lastly, good code is also *maintainable*, meaning that its individual parts can be updated without fear of compromising the integrity of the whole.

In contrast, coding this same effect in jQuery would entail the following:

```
$div
  // Register a mouseover event on this div, which calls an animation
  → function
  .on("mouseover", function() {
    $(this).animate({ color: "blue" }, 200);
  })
  // When the user hovers off the element, animate the text color back
  → to black
  .on("mouseout", function() {
    // Note: We have to remember what the original property value
    → was (black)
    $(this).animate({ color: "black" }, 200);
  });
```

This might not look so bad, but the code isn't taking advantage of the fact that JavaScript provides an infinite amount of logical control. It goes out of its way to do something that CSS is designed for: triggering logicless animations that occur on the same element that the user is interacting with. Above, you're doing in JavaScript what you could have done in fewer, more expressive, and more maintainable lines of CSS. Even worse, you're not getting any additional feature benefits by implementing this functionality in JavaScript.

In short, if you can easily use CSS transitions to animate an element that's never being animated by JavaScript (meaning there's no potential for conflict), then you *should* code that animation in CSS. For all other UI animation tasks—multi-element and multistep sequences, interactive drag animations, and much more—JavaScript animation is the superior solution.

Let's explore the fantastic workflow techniques JavaScript provides.

CODE TECHNIQUE: SEPARATE STYLING FROM LOGIC

The first technique has profound workflow benefits, especially for teams.

STANDARD APPROACH

In jQuery animation, it's common to animate CSS classes onto elements using the UI add-on plugin (jQueryUI.com). When the module is loaded, jQuery's addClass() and removeClass() functions are upgraded with animation support. For example, let's say you have a CSS class defined in a stylesheet as follows:

```
.fadeInAndMove {
    opacity: 1;
    top: 50px;
}
```

You can then animate the CSS properties of that class (opacity and top in this case) onto the target element along with a specified duration:

```
// Animate the properties of the .fadeInAndMove class over a
→ 1000ms duration
$element.addClass("fadeInAndMove", 1000);
```

The more common implementation of jQuery animation consists of inlining the desired animation properties within an $.animate() call, which uses the syntax demonstrated in Chapter 1, "Advantages of JavaScript Animation":

```
$element.animate({ opacity: 1, top: 50 }, 1000);
```

Both implementations produce the same result. The difference is their *separation of logic*: The first implementation delegates the styling rules to a CSS stylesheet, where the rest of the page's styling rules reside. The second mixes styling rules with the JavaScript logic responsible for triggering them.

The first approach is preferable due to the organizational cleanliness and flexibility gained by knowing where to look to make the appropriate style or logic changes to your code. CSS stylesheets exist for a reason; seasoned developers do not inline CSS into their HTML. That would conflate the purposes of HTML (structure) and CSS (styling), and make a site considerably more difficult to maintain.

The value of logic separation is further pronounced when working in a team environment, in which it's common for developers and designers to bump heads while trying to edit the same file at the same time.

OPTIMIZED APPROACH

With the review of standard methods out of the way, let's look at the optimized approach. It's just as beneficial—and often the best methodology for JavaScript-centric animation workflows—to shift animation styling logic into a dedicated JavaScript file (for example, a *style.js*) rather than a dedicated CSS stylesheet. Sounds weird, right? Perhaps, but it works **brilliantly**. This technique leverages plain old JavaScript objects to help you organize your animation code.

For example, your *style.js* file might look like this:

```
// This object is a parallel to the CSS class defined in the previous
→ code example
var fadeIn = {
    opacity: 1,
    top: "50px"
};
```

In your *script.js*, which is the primary JavaScript file that controls animation logic, you would then have:

```
// Pass our named properties object into Velocity
$element.velocity(fadeIn, 1000);
```

To recap, in your *style.js*, you've defined a JavaScript object that's populated with the CSS properties you want to animate. This is the same object that's then passed into Velocity as a first argument. You're not doing anything fancy here—just saving objects to named variables, then passing those variables into Velocity instead of the raw objects themselves.

NOTE: This technique works equally well with jQuery's `animate()` function.

a pain-free workflow is vital.

The benefit of switching from CSS to JavaScript to segregate logic is that your *style.js* file is uniquely capable of defining animation *options*—not just animation properties. There are many ways to specify an option: one is to assign two member properties to a parent animation object to which you assign an expressive name. The first property on the object defines the animation's properties; the second defines its options.

In this case, your *style.js* file would look like this:

```
var fadeIn = {
    // p is for "properties"
    p: {
      opacity: 1,
      top: "50px"
    },
    // o is for "options"
    o: {
      duration: 1000,
      easing: "linear"
    }
};
```

In the *script.js* file, you'd have:

```
// Pass in our clean and re-usable animation objects
$element.velocity(fadeIn.p, fadeIn.o);
```

Pretty and clean, right? Someone skimming it would understand its purpose, and would know where to look to modify its properties—the *style.js* file. Further, the purpose of this animation is immediately evident: because you've named the animation object appropriately, you know that the code serves to *fade* an object into view. You no longer have to mentally parse animation properties to assess the purpose of the animation.

This approach discourages you from arbitrarily setting options for each individual animation on a page since there's now a bank of premade animation objects you can easily pull from. This results in leaner code and more consistent motion design. Consistency, as you learned in the previous chapter, is a key component of great UX.

But the best part is that this approach lends itself perfectly to organizing your animation *variations* together. For example, if you typically fade button elements into view with a duration of 1000ms, but you fade modal windows into view with a duration of 3000ms, you can simply split your options object into two appropriately named variations:

```
var fadeIn = {
    p: {
        opacity: 1,
        top: "50px"
    },
    // Options object variation #1 uses a fast duration
    oFast: {
        duration: 1000,
        easing: "linear"
    },
    // Variation #2 uses a slower duration
    oSlow: {
        duration: 3000,
        easing: "linear"
    }
};
// Animate using the fast duration.
$button.velocity(fadeIn.p, fadeIn.oFast);
/* Animate using the slow duration. */
$modal.velocity(fadeIn.p, fadeIn.oSlow);
```

Alternatively, you could nest "fast" and "slow" objects as children of a singular o options object. The choice of which implementation to use is based on your personal preference:

```
var fadeIn = {
    p: {
        opacity: 1,
        top: "50px"
    },
    o: {
        fast: {
            duration: 1000,
            easing: "linear"
        },
        slow: {
            duration: 3000,
            easing: "linear"
        }
    }
};
// Animate using the fast duration.
$button.velocity(fadeIn.p, fadeIn.o.fast);
/* Animate using the slow duration. */
$modal.velocity(fadeIn.p, fadeIn.o.slow);
```

If this seems like too much overhead, and if you have few enough lines of JavaScript to justify simply inlining all your animation logic, then don't feel like a bad developer for skipping this approach altogether. You should always use whichever degree of abstraction best suits the scope of your project. The takeaway here is simply that animation workflow best practices do exist if you find yourself needing them.

CODE TECHNIQUE: ORGANIZE SEQUENCED ANIMATIONS

Velocity has a small add-on plugin called the *UI pack* (get it at VelocityJS.org/#uiPack). It enhances Velocity with features that greatly improve the UI animation workflow. Many of the techniques in this chapter, including the one discussed below, make use of it.

To install the UI pack, simply include a `<script>` tag for it after Velocity and before the ending `</body>` tag of your page:

```
<script src="velocity.js"></script>
<script src="velocity.ui.js"></script>
```

The specific UI pack feature discussed in this section is called *sequence running*. It will forever change your animation workflow. It is the solution to messily nested animation code.

STANDARD APPROACH

Without the UI pack, the standard approach to consecutively animating separate elements is as follows:

```
// Animate element1 followed by element2 followed by element3
$element1.velocity({ translateX: 100, opacity: 1 }, 1000, function() {
  $element2.velocity({ translateX: 200, opacity: 1 }, 1000, function() {
    $element3.velocity({ translateX: 300, opacity: 1 }, 1000);
  });
});
```

Don't let this simple example fool you: in real-world production code, animation sequences include many more properties, many more options, and many more levels of nesting than are demonstrated here. Code like this most commonly appears in loading sequences (when a page or a subsection first loads in) that consist of multiple elements animating into place.

Note that the code shown above is different from chaining multiple animations onto the *same* element, which is hassle-free and doesn't require nesting:

```
// Chain multiple animations onto the same element
$element1
    .velocity({ translateX: 100 })
    .velocity({ translateY: 100 })
    .velocity({ translateZ: 100 });
```

So what's wrong with first code sample (the one with different elements)? Here are the main issues:

- The code bloats horizontally very quickly with each level of nesting, making it increasingly difficult to modify the code within your IDE.
- You can't easily rearrange the order of calls in the overall sequence (doing so requires very delicate copying and pasting).
- You can't easily indicate that certain calls should run parallel to one another. Let's say that halfway through the overall sequence you want two images to slide into view from different origin points. When coding this in, it wouldn't be obvious how to nest animations that occur after this parallel mini-sequence such that the overall sequence doesn't become even more difficult to maintain than it already is.

OPTIMIZED APPROACH

Before you learn about the beautiful solution to this ugly problem, it's important to understand two simple features of Velocity. First, know that Velocity accepts multiple argument syntaxes: the most common, when Velocity is invoked on a jQuery element object (like all the code examples shown so far), consists of a properties object followed by an options object:

```
// The argument syntax used thus far
$element.velocity({ opacity: 1, top: "50px" }, { duration: 1000,
→ easing: "linear" });
```

An alternative syntax pairs with Velocity's *utility function*, which is the fancy name given to animating elements using the base Velocity object instead of chaining off of a jQuery element object. Here's what animating off the base Velocity object looks like:

```
// Velocity registers itself on jQuery's $ object, which you leverage here
$.Velocity({ e: $element, p: { opacity: 1, scale: 1 },
→ o: { duration: 1000, easing: "linear" } });
```

As shown above, this alternative syntax consists of passing Velocity a *single object* that contains member objects that map to each of the standard Velocity arguments (*elements*, *properties*, and *options*). For the sake of brevity, the member object names are truncated to the first letter of their associated objects (e for elements, p for properties, and o for options).

Further, note that you're now passing the target element in as an argument to Velocity since you're no longer invoking Velocity directly on the element. The net effect is exactly the same as the syntax you used earlier.

As you can see, the new syntax isn't much bulkier, but it's equally—if not more—expressive. Armed with this new syntax, you're ready to learn how the UI pack's sequence-running feature works: you simply create an array of Velocity calls, with each call defined using the single-object syntax just demonstrated. You then pass the entire array into a special Velocity function that fires the sequence's calls successively. When one Velocity call is completed, the next runs—even if the individual calls are targeting different elements:

```
// Create the array of Velocity calls
var loadingSequence = [
    { e: $element1, p: { translateX: 100, opacity: 1 },
    ⇒ o: { duration: 1000 } },
    { e: $element2, p: { translateX: 200, opacity: 1 },
    ⇒ o: { duration: 1000 } },
    { e: $element3, p: { translateX: 300, opacity: 1 },
    ⇒ o: { duration: 1000 } }
];
// Pass the array into $.Velocity.RunSequence to kick off the sequence
$.Velocity.RunSequence(loadingSequence);
```

The benefits here are clear:

- You can easily reorder animations in the overall sequence without fear of breaking nested code.
- You can quickly eyeball the difference between properties and options objects across the calls.
- Your code is highly legible and expressive to others.

If you combine this technique with the previous technique (turning CSS classes into JavaScript objects), your animation code starts to look remarkably elegant:

```
$.Velocity.RunSequence([
    { e: $element1, p: { translateX: 100, opacity: 1 }, o: slideIn.o },
    { e: $element2, p: { translateX: 200, opacity: 1 }, o: slideIn.o },
    { e: $element3, p: { translateX: 300, opacity: 1 }, o: slideIn.o }
]);
```

Expressiveness and maintainability aren't the only benefits to sequence running: you also gain the ability to run individual calls in parallel using a special sequenceQueue option which, when set to *false*, forces the associated call to run parallel to the call that came before it. This lets you have multiple elements animate into view simultaneously, giving a single Velocity sequence the power to intricately control timing that would normally have to be orchestrated through messy callback nesting. Refer to the inlined comments below for details:

```
$.Velocity.RunSequence([
    { elements: $element1, properties: { translateX: 100 },
    → options: { duration: 1000 } },
    // The following call will start at the same time as the first
    → call since it uses the `sequenceQueue: false` option
    { elements: $element2, properties: { translateX: 200 },
    → options: { duration: 1000, sequenceQueue: false },
    // As normal, the call below will run once the second call has completed
    { elements: $element3, properties: { translateX: 300 },
    → options: { duration: 1000 }
];
```

CODE TECHNIQUE: PACKAGE YOUR EFFECTS

One of the most common uses of motion design is fading content in and out of view. This type of animation often consists of a series of individual animation calls that are chained together to deliver a nuanced, multistage effect.

STANDARD APPROACH

Instead of simply animating the opacity of an element toward 1, you might simultaneously animate its *scale* property so that the element appears to both fade in and grow into place. Once the element is fully in view, you might choose to animate its border thickness to 1rem as a finishing touch. If this animation were to happen multiple times across a page, and on many different elements, it would make sense to avoid code repetition by turning it into a standalone function. Otherwise, you'd have to repeat this non-expressive code throughout your *script.js*:

```
$element
    .velocity({ opacity: 1, scale: 1 }, { duration: 500,
    → easing: "ease-in-out" })
    .velocity({ borderWidth: "1rem" }, { delay: 200,
    → easing: "spring", duration: 400 });
```

Unlike the sequencing technique discussed in the previous section, the code above consists of multiple animations that all occur on the *same* element. Chained animations on a singular element constitute an **effect**. If you were to improve this effect by implementing the first technique in this chapter (turning CSS classes into JavaScript objects), you'd have to go out of your way to uniquely name each argument object for each stage in the overall animation. Not only is it possible that these objects wouldn't be used by other portions of the animation code due to the uniqueness of this particular sequence, but you'd have to deal with appending integers to each animation call's respective objects to delineate them from one another. This could get messy, and could neutralize the organizational benefit and brevity of turning CSS classes into JavaScript objects.

Another problem with effects such as the one above is that the code isn't very self-descriptive—its purpose isn't immediately clear. Why are there two animation calls instead of one? What is the reasoning behind the choice of properties and options for each of these individual calls? The answers to these questions are irrelevant to the code that triggers the animation, and should consequently be tucked away.

OPTIMIZED APPROACH

Velocity's UI pack lets you register effects that you can subsequently reuse across a site. Once an effect is registered, you can call it by passing its name into Velocity as its first parameter:

```
// Assume we registered our effect under the name "growIn"
$element.velocity("growIn");
```

That's a lot more expressive, isn't it? You quickly understand the code's purpose: An element will grow into view. The code remains terse and maintainable.

What's more, a registered effect behaves identically to a standard Velocity call; you can pass in an options object as normal and chain other Velocity calls onto it:

```
$element
    // Scroll the element into view
    .velocity("scroll")
    // Then trigger the "growIn" effect on it, with the following settings
    .velocity("growIn", { duration: 1000, delay: 200 })
```

If the UI pack is loaded onto your page, an effect such as this is registered using the following syntax:

```
$.Velocity.RegisterEffect(name, {
    // Default duration value if one isn't passed into the call
    defaultDuration: duration,
    // The following Velocity calls occur one after another,
    → with each taking up
    a predefined percentage of the effect's total duration
    calls: [
        [ propertiesObject, durationPercentage, optionsObject ] ,
        [ propertiesObject, durationPercentage, optionsObject ]
    ],
    reset: resetPropertiesObject
});
```

Let's break down this template step by step:

1. The first argument is the name of the effect. If the effect is responsible for bringing an element into view (as in, it fades an element's opacity from 0 to 1), it's important to suffix the effect with "In".

2. The second argument is an object that defines the effect's behavior. The first property in this object is defaultDuration, which lets you specify the duration the full effect should take if one is not passed into the Velocity call that triggers the effect.

3. The next property in the object is the calls array, which consists of the Velocity calls that constitute the effect (in the order that they should occur). Each of these array items is an array itself, which consists of the call's properties object, followed by the optional percentage of the total duration which that call should consume (a decimal value that defaults to 1.00), followed by an optional options object for that specific call. Note that Velocity calls specified within the calls array accept only the easing and delay options.

4. Finally, you have the option of passing in a reset object. The reset object is specified using the same syntax as a standard Velocity properties map object, but it is used to enact an immediate value change upon completion of the full effect. This is useful when you're animating the opacity and scale properties of an element down to 0 (out of view), but want to return the element's scale property to 1 after the element is hidden so that subsequent effects needn't worry about the properties beyond opacity they must reset on the element for their calls to properly take effect. In other words, you can leverage the *reset* properties map to make effects self-contained, such that they leave no clean up duties on the target elements.

In addition to the *reset* object, another powerful workflow bonus of the UI pack's effect registration is automatic display property toggling. When an element begins animating into view, you want to ensure its display value is set to a value other than "none" so the element is visible throughout the course of its animation. (Remember, display: none removes an element from the page's flow.) Conversely, when fading an element out, you often want to ensure its display value is switched to "none" once its opacity hits 0. This way, you remove all traces of the element when you're done using it.

Using jQuery, *display* toggling is accomplished by chaining the show() and hide() helper functions onto animations (oftentimes messily buried within nested callbacks). With Velocity's UI pack, however, this logic is taken care of automatically when you suffix your effect names with "In" and "Out" as appropriate.

Let's register two UI pack effects—one for the "In" direction and one for the "Out" direction—and call the element "shadowIn" since it consists of fading and scaling an element into view, then expanding its boxShadow property outward:

```
$.Velocity
  .RegisterEffect("shadowIn", {
    defaultDuration: 1000,
    calls: [
      [ { opacity: 1, scale: 1 }, 0.4 ] ,
      [ { boxShadowBlur: 50 }, 0.6 ]
    ]
})
  .RegisterEffect("shadowOut", {
    defaultDuration: 800,
    calls: [
      // We reverse the order to mirror the "In" direction
      [ { boxShadowBlur: 50 }, 0.2 ],
      [ { opacity: 0, scale: 0 }, 0.8 ]
    ]
});
```

If your effect's name ends with "Out", Velocity will automatically set the element's display property to "none" once the animation is complete. Conversely, if your effect's name ends with "In", Velocity will automatically set the element's display property to the default value associated with the element's tag type (for example, "inline" for anchors, "block" for div and p). If your effect's name does not contain one of these special suffixes, the UI pack will not perform automatic display setting.

Registering effects not only improves your code, but also makes it highly portable between projects and among fellow developers. When you've designed an effect you love, now it's painless to share the effect's registration code with others so they can use it too. Pretty neat!

DESIGN TECHNIQUES

The techniques discussed so far in this chapter will improve your workflow during the *coding* phase of motion design. The techniques covered in this section focus on the *design* phase, where you're still experimenting to find the perfect animation that fits your UI. This phase requires a lot of creativity and a lot of repetition, and is accordingly ripe for workflow improvements.

TIMING MULTIPLIERS

The first design technique is to use a *global timing multiplier*. This consists of sprinkling in a multiplier constant against all of your animations' *delay* and *duration* values.

Start by defining your global timing multiplier (arbitrarily designated as M for multiplier):

```
var M = 1;
```

Then, bake the multiplier into the duration and delay option values within each animation call:

```
$element1.animate({ opacity: 1 }, { duration: 1000 * M });
$element2.velocity({ opacity: 1 }, { delay: 250 * M });
```

> **NOTE:** if you use SASS or LESS, which provide support for variable usage within stylesheets, this technique applies equally to CSS animations!

Embedding a multiplier constant will help you quickly modify the M constant in one location (presumably at the top of your *style.js*) in order to quickly speed up or slow down all of the animations across your page. Benefits of such timing control include:

- Slowing down animations to perfect the timing of individual animation calls within a complex animation sequence. When you're constantly refreshing your page in order to tweak a multi-element animation sequence to perfection, seeing the sequence in slow motion makes it significantly easier to assess how individual elements interact with one another.

- Speeding up animations when you're performing repetitive UI testing. When you're testing a site for purposes *other* than animation, evaluating the *end state* of UI animations (how elements wind up) is more important than testing the animations' motion. In these situations, it saves time and reduces headaches to speed up all the animations across your page so you're not repeatedly waiting for your animations to play out on each page refresh.

Velocity has a handy implementation of this functionality called *mock,* which functions as a behind-the-scenes global multiplier so you don't have to sprinkle in the M constant by hand. Like the example shown above, mock multiplies both the duration and the delay values. To turn mock on, temporarily set $.Velocity.mock to the multiplier value you want to use:

```
// Multiply all animation timing by 5
$.Velocity.mock = 5;
// All animations are now time-adjusted
// The duration below effectively becomes 5000ms
$element.velocity({ opacity: 1 }, { duration: 1000 });
```

Velocity's mock feature also accepts a Boolean value: setting mock to *true* sets all durations and delays to oms, which forces all animations to complete within a single browser timing tick, which occurs every few milliseconds. This is a powerful shortcut for quickly turning off all animations when they're getting in the way of your UI development and testing.

USE VELOCITY MOTION DESIGNER

Velocity Motion Designer (VMD) was crafted with the sole purpose of helping developers streamline the creation phase of motion design. VMD is a bookmarklet that you load onto a page in order to design animations in real time. It allows you to double-click elements to open a modal that lets you specify animation properties and options for that element. You then hit Enter on your keyboard to watch the animation play out immediately—without a page refresh.

NOTE: Get Velocity Motion Designer at http://velocityjs.org/#vmd.

make motion design fun.

Once you've designed all your element animations exactly the way you want them, you can export your work into one-for-one Velocity code, which you can place immediately into an IDE for use in production. (The resulting code is also fully compatible with jQuery.)

Ultimately, VMD saves countless hours of development time by preventing constant IDE and browser tab switching and repeated UI state retriggering. Further, it streamlines the designer-to-developer workflow by allowing the two teams to work alongside one another in real time: with VMD, designers can implement motion design without having to familiarize themselves with a site's JavaScript or CSS. They can simply hand off the exported Velocity code to the developers to integrate into the codebase at their discretion.

VMD is a highly visual tool—visit VelocityJS.org/#vmd to see the walkthrough video.

WRAPPING UP

As you implement animation workflow techniques, you'll notice the intimidating black box of motion design beginning to unfold. The beautifully intricate loading sequences found on cutting-edge sites like Stripe.com and Webflow.com will start to make sense to you. You'll gain confidence in your ability to code animation sequences, and this newfound skill will reduce friction in your development routine, making it not only easier but also significantly more fun to accomplish your motion design goals.

CHAPTER 5

Animating Text

Since textual animation is rarely employed in webpages, using it is an easy way to impress users. That's precisely what makes this topic so much fun to learn: the underlying techniques are simple to program, but the results feel incredibly rich and complex to the user.

This chapter introduces you to tools that remove the tedious aspects of textual animation and equip you with an efficient workflow. Read on to learn the nuances of this dark art.

THE STANDARD APPROACH
TO TEXT ANIMATION

The standard HTML elements we code sites with—divs, tables, anchor tags, and the like—are the lowest-level components of a webpage that can be styled. So it makes sense that these are the lowest-level components that can be animated.

Text does not constitute an element unto itself; a block of text is designated by the browser as a *text node*, which is an unstylable, lower-level component that must be *contained* by an element. Further complicating matters is the fact that the browser does not subdivide text nodes into grammatical components; there is no way to access individual letters, words, or sentences.

Consequently, to animate text on a letter, word, or sentence basis, you have to break each text node into separate text nodes, and then wrap each of these in a new element. You can then animate them. But manually wrapping text in *span* elements, for example, is tedious work that results in bloated HTML.

It's no surprise then that text animation on the web is uncommon; it's typically too much of a hassle to deal with. This puts the web at an aesthetic disadvantage to dedicated motion design software, such as Adobe After Effects, which allows for the fine-grained animation of text—the results of which are commonly seen in TV commercials and movie title sequences. These effects can look absolutely beautiful. Unfortunately, in addition to being difficult to integrate on the web, they're also widely considered bad practice. After all, the web is a medium that prioritizes function over form, and text animation is largely about form.

However, there is one textual animation use case that can carry over well to the web when used sparingly: if you pay close attention to the depictions of futuristic hardware interfaces in movies, you'll notice the common thread of text being animated into or out of view on a *grammatical* level. The future of computing, according to pop culture, consists of words and sentences animating with flickers, glitches, pops, and blurs. These effects look cool, and there isn't much downside to embracing them for the purposes of transitioning content into or out of view since the text had to undergo a visibility animation by one means or another. This concept of transitioning text visibility is precisely what you'll learn about in this chapter.

text effects look plain cool.

PREPARING TEXT ELEMENTS FOR ANIMATION WITH BLAST.JS

The tool of choice for typographic animation is Blast.js, which handily breaks blocks of text into characters, words, and sentences. You can then animate the resulting parts using Velocity and its UI pack plugin.

NOTE: Get Blast.js at Julian.com/research/blast.

Blast.js has three delimiter types to define the grammatical components to be individually extracted: character, word, and sentence. Suppose you have a div that looks like this:

```
<div>
   Hello World
</div>
```

If you call Blast on this div using the following syntax

```
$("div").blast({ delimiter: "word" });
```

the div would turn into this:

```
<div class="blast-root">
   <span class="blast">Hello</span>
   <span class="blast">World</span>
</div>
```

As you can see, Blast separated the target div's text into text parts that are individually wrapped in span elements. If you were to instead use the character delimiter, the result would have been:

```
<div class="blast-root">
   <span class="blast">H</span>
   <span class="blast">e</span>
   <span class="blast">l</span>
   <span class="blast">l</span>
   <span class="blast">o</span>
```

```
<span class="blast"> </span>
<span class="blast">W</span>
<span class="blast">o</span>
<span class="blast">r</span>
<span class="blast">l</span>
<span class="blast">d</span>
</div>
```

You can now animate these span elements independently. Before you dive into textual animation, however, you're going to learn more about how Blast works so you can take full advantage of its powerful features.

HOW BLAST.JS WORKS

The goal of this section is to make you comfortable with the prospect of using Blast to break apart the text on your beloved page. Let's dive in!

divs, tables, and the other HTML elements that you're familiar with are called *element nodes.* An element node commonly consists of two types of children: additional element nodes and text nodes (raw text).

Take this element, for example:

```
<div>
  Hello <span>World</span>
</div>
```

This div element is composed of two children: a text node ("Hello") and a span element node. The span element node contains a child of its own: another text node ("World").

When Blast is called, it traverses the entirety of the target element's descendant element chain to find text nodes. With each text node, Blast executes the RegEx query associated with the specified delimiter type (character, word, or sentence) to subdivide the node into new elements, each with its own text node part. Since Blast doesn't actually subdivide *element* nodes—only text nodes—you can safely apply it to the entire page without worrying about breaking elements' event handlers and other expected behaviors. This versatility is crucial when using Blast on user-generated content that is often dirtied with HTML. (Say, for example, you want to separate the words in a message posted to your site's comments section so you can highlight important passages. With Blast, you can safely do so without concern for breaking the user's embedded links.)

In addition to its robustness, Blast provides a high level of accuracy. It doesn't dumbly split words at spaces, nor does it split sentences at periods within words. It leverages UTF-8 character sets for Latin alphabet languages, meaning that you can accurately apply it to French, German, Spanish, English, Italian, and Portuguese content.

Suppose you used Blast's sentence delimiter on the following paragraph. (**Bold** and *italic* are used below to indicate the consecutive text matches that Blast detects.) Blast correctly identified six sentences in the paragraph:

¿Will the sentence delimiter recognize this full sentence containing Spanish punctuation? *¡Yes!* **« Mais, oui ! »** "Nested "quotes" don't break the sentence delimiter!" *Further, periods inside words (e.g. Blast.js), in formal titles (e.g. Mrs. Bluth, Dr. Fünke), and in "e.g." and "i.e." do not falsely match as sentence-final punctuation.* **Darn.** *That's pretty impressive.*

Notice how punctuation is associated with its proper sentence, and how errant periods don't falsely demarcate sentence matches.

With these foundations covered, it's time to run through how to use Blast.

INSTALLATION

Blast is installed on a page like any other JavaScript plugin: embed the appropriate script link before your page's `</body>` tag:

```
<html>
    <head>My Page</head>
    <body>
        My content.
        <script src="jquery.js"></script>
        <script src="velocity.js"></script>
        <script src="blast.js"></script>
    </body>
</html>
```

NOTE: Blast requires jQuery (or Zepto, a jQuery alternative), and therefore must be required after jQuery. It doesn't matter whether Blast is loaded before or after Velocity.

Once Blast is loaded, use it by calling `.blast()` on a jQuery element object. It accepts an options object as its sole argument:

```
$element.blast({ option1: value1, option2: value2 });
```

Let's run through the available options.

OPTION: DELIMITER

Blast's most important option is `delimiter`, which accepts `"character"`, `"word"`, or `"sentence"`. To separate the text within `$element` using the `"sentence"` delimiter, your code would look like this:

```
$element.blast({ delimiter: "sentence" });
```

Note that Blast returns the generated text wrapper elements to the jQuery selector chain so you can manipulate them, like this:

```
$element.blast({ delimiter: "sentence" })
  .css("opacity", 0.5);
```

The `.css()` call is applied to the individual text elements, not the parent `$element` that you called Blast on.

OPTION: CUSTOMCLASS

Blast provides two options to make text manipulation easier: `customClass` and `generateValueClass`. `customClass` behaves exactly as you would expect: supply a custom class (as a string value) to be assigned to the text node wrapper elements.

Suppose you had the following div and Blast call:

```
<div>
  Hi Mom
</div>
$("div").blast({ delimiter: "word" , customClass: "myClass" });
```

The div would turn into the following (note how Blast automatically assigns every text part the "blast" class by default):

```
<div>
    <span class="blast myClass">Hi</span>
    <span class="blast myClass">Mom</span>
</div>
```

The value in providing a custom class is in differentiating the elements generated by each Blast call. If, for example, you used Blast in two locations on your page—once in the header and once in the footer—it might be helpful to assign these two calls different classes so your subsequent JavaScript code and CSS styles can act on the text elements appropriately.

OPTION: GENERATEVALUECLASS

generateValueClass takes a Boolean value (true or false) indicating whether a unique class, in the form of .blast-[delimiter]-[textValue], should be assigned to the generated text elements.

NOTE: This option is applicable only to the character and word delimiters.

The [delimiter] placeholder represents the delimiter type used in the call, and the [textValue] placeholder represents the text contained within an individual element. Consider the following example:

```
<div>
    Hi Mom
</div>
$("div").blast({ delimiter: "word" , generateValueClass: true });
```

The element would turn into this:

```
<div class="blast-root">
    <span class="blast blast-word-Hi">Hi</span>
    <span class="blast blast-word-Mom">Mom</span>
</div>
```

When Blast is called with the `letter` delimiter, the element would turn into this instead:

```
<div class="blast-root">
   <span class="blast blast-letter-H">H</span>
   <span class="blast blast-letter-i">i</span>
   ... and so on...
</div>
```

The generateValueClass option is useful when you need to use CSS or JavaScript to manipulate text matches based on the text contained with them. If, for example, you used this feature on a book excerpt, you could create a visualization of all instances of the word "and" by giving elements with the `.blast.word-and` class a yellow background:

```
// jQuery implementation
$(".blast-word-and").css("background", "yellow");
// Raw JavaScript implementation
document.querySelectorAll(".blast-word-and").forEach(function(item)
→ { item.style.background = "yellow"; });
// CSS implementation
.blast-word-and {
   background: yellow;
}
```

Thanks to this feature, you can painlessly target text matches via either CSS or JavaScript without having to use messy custom code to individually check the text contents of each element.

OPTION: TAG

This option lets you specify the type of element that wraps text parts. The default value is span, but you can pass in any element type (for example, a, div, p). Consider this example:

```
<div>
   Hi Mom
</div>
// Use the "div" element as the wrapper tag
$("div").blast({ delimiter: "word" , tag: "div" });
```

The element would consequently turn into this:

```
<div class="blast-root">
   <div class="blast">Hi</div>
   <div class="blast">Mom</div>
</div>
```

This feature is useful to ensure that the resulting text elements mimic the structure of the surrounding HTML. Perhaps nearby sibling elements are all of the div type, in which case the above example may be appropriate.

You might also want to take advantage of the unique properties offered by different tag types. strong, for example, automatically bolds text, whereas div forces each text match to begin on a new line thanks to div's default display value of "block".

COMMAND: REVERSE

You can undo Blast on an element by passing false as the sole parameter into a Blast call. Hence, if your Blasted element looked like this:

```
<div class="blast-root">
   <div class="blast">Hi</div>
   <div class="blast">Mom</div>
</div>
```

and you passed in the following Blast call:

```
$("div").blast(false);
```

the element would return to its original structure:

```
<div>
   Hi Mom
</div>
```

You might be wondering how this works: when Blast is reversed, it simply destroys the generated wrapper elements, then inserts raw text where the wrapper elements were previously. Note that this will break event handlers assigned to the new elements generated by Blast, but it won't break event handlers associated with the HTML that existed prior to Blast being initially called.

Reversing Blast in this way is a crucial component of textual animation since the modus operandi when animating elements on a webpage is to leave things as they were before you touched them. If, for example, you've Blasted apart a sentence in order to animate its words into view one at a time, you would subsequently reverse Blast upon completion of the animation. Consequently, JavaScript code that later interacts with the text won't have unexpected child elements that it has to parse out. In short, it's good practice to avoid leaving your HTML unnecessarily bloated so that further programmatic interaction with your elements doesn't become increasingly convoluted.

NOTE: To learn more about Blast, including its unique search capabilities and its compatibility with screen-reading software, visit its documentation at Julian.com/research/blast.

Now that you've separated your text elements, it's time to animate them.

TRANSITIONING TEXT INTO OR OUT OF VIEW

The most common use of textual animation is animating text in and out of view. A basic implementation of this is to animate the words in a sentence into view one after another.

REPLACING EXISTING TEXT

Let's start by creating a container div with placeholder text that will be replaced by new text that animates into place:

```
<div>
    A message will load here shortly...
</div>
```

Because the div starts out as visible, Blasting the div's text results in child text elements that are visible as well. Since your goal is to animate the generated text elements into view starting from a state of *invisibility*, you have to make the generated text elements invisible immediately after you call Blast:

```
$("div")
    .html("This is our new message.")
    .blast({ delimiter: "word" })
        .css("opacity", 0);
        .velocity({ opacity: 1 });
```

This replaces the div's existing text with a new message. Then it Blasts the div using the word delimiter. Since a call to Blast returns the generated text wrapper elements to the jQuery selector chain, you can easily extend the code to set the opacity of each text element to 0. This primes the elements for the subsequent Velocity call, which consists of a simple opacity animation.

You may have noticed that the above code results in all text parts animating into view simultaneously. This, of course, defeats the purpose of using Blast in the first place: if you wanted all of the div's content to animate into view simultaneously, you could have simply animated the div itself. The goal here is actually to achieve a successive animation sequence that consists of one text element animating after another.

STAGGERING

This is where Velocity's UI pack comes into play. (Review Chapter 4, "Animation Workflow," if you need a primer on the UI pack.) To impose a successive delay between animation start times within an element set, use Velocity UI pack's stagger option, which expects a duration specified in milliseconds. Applying it to the previous code example, you get:

```
$("div")
  .html("This is our new message.")
  .blast({ delimiter: "word" })
    .css("opacity", 0)
    .velocity("transition.fadeIn", { stagger: 50 });
```

The code above produces a successive delay of 50ms between the elements' animation start times. Importantly, note the Velocity call's previous { opacity: 1 } argument for "transition.fadeIn", which is a premade fade effect included with Velocity's UI pack. (Refer to Chapter 4, "Animation Workflow," if you need a refresher.) Since the stagger option works with UI pack effects, this example shows the effect that mirrors animating opacity to a value only of 1.

As discussed in Chapter 3, "Motion Design Theory," be careful to keep stagger times to a low duration so that users aren't waiting needlessly while text fades into view. Keep in mind that the longer an element's word count, the greater the overall time an animation sequence will take to complete. Text element staggering is one of the easiest ways to slip into the bad practice of slowing down your interface.

TRANSITIONING TEXT OUT OF VIEW

The code example in the previous section only animated text into—not out of—view; the div's preexisting text was immediately replaced by the new message. This doesn't necessarily make for poor motion design, but it is often beneficial from the perspective of motion design theory to unify animations such that an element fades out of view in a way that reflects the way it faded into view. Chapter 3, "Motion Design Theory," covered the concept of *mirroring* animations so that what comes in reflects what goes out. That advice applies here.

If you want the outward textual animation to mirror the inward animation, you could rework the code example as follows:

```
// Select the previously blasted text
$("div .blast").velocity(
    // Animate the existing text out of view with the appropriate
    ⇒ UI pack effect
    "transition.fadeOut",
    {
        // Stagger the outward animation as you did the inward animation
        stagger: 50,
        backwards: true,
        // When this outward animation is complete, begin the inward animation
        complete: function() {
            // Proceed with the inward animation
            $("div")
                .html(message)
                .blast({ delimiter: "word" })
                    .css("opacity", 0)
                    .velocity({ opacity: 1 }, { stagger: 50 });
        }
    }
);
```

This begins by calling the Velocity UI pack "transition.fadeOut" effect on the text parts generated by the div having previously been Blasted. As with the inward direction, the stagger option successively offsets the individual text part animations in the outward direction. New to this call is the use of Velocity UI pack's backwards option, which pairs with stagger to reverse the target element set's order so that the last element (the last word in the sentence) animates out of view before the second-to-last element does, and that element animates out of view before the third-to-last element does, and so on. When this outward animation sequence is complete, the inward animation is called from within the complete callback.

Using the `backwards` option for text animation provides two benefits. First, it helps mirror (create the inverse of) the inward animation, which consists of the first word animating into view before the second word does, and so on. Second, when the backward animation is immediately followed by the forward animation, the net result is an elegant chaining effect in which the last word in the backward direction and the first word in the forward direction occur back-to-back. This works to tie the two animation sequences together into what looks like one conjoined animation instead of two separate animations crudely glued together.

TRANSITIONING INDIVIDUAL TEXT PARTS

Movie title sequences are well known for their inventive typographic motion design. The technique underlying many of these effects is singling out individual text elements for animation. That's what this section covers.

NOTE: For typographic animation inspiration, search YouTube for movie title sequences and take detailed notes! As long as you keep the principles of motion design theory in mind, you should feel encouraged to explore textual animation design in your interface.

To achieve fine-grained control over the elements that Blast generates, simply use CSS's nth-child selector or jQuery's eq() function. These functions behave similarly to one another, in that they allow for the selection of an element within a set based on that element's index. If you passed an integer value of 3 into these functions (or 2 in the case of jQuery as you will see), they would target the third element (that is, third word) in the full element set (that is, multiword sentence):

```
// CSS implementation
.blast:nth-child(3) {
   color: red;
}
// jQuery implementation
$(".blast").eq(2).css("color", "red");
```

Both examples above target the third element on the page that has the .blast class applied. (Note that jQuery's eq function is 0-based whereas CSS' nth-child is 1-based, hence the different integer values being passed into the examples.) Let's continue with a jQuery implementation to work toward a complete example:

```
<div>
    Current status: paused
</div>
// Blast the div using the word delimiter
$("div").blast({ delimiter: "word" })
        // Select the third word in the sentence (the span containing
    ⇥ the "paused" text)
        .eq(2)
            // Fade the third element out of view then replace its inner
        ⇥ text with a new message
            .velocity({ opacity: 0 }, function() { $(this).text("running"); })
            // Fade the replaced text into view
            .velocity({ opacity: 1 });
```

This Blasts a sentence, selects its third word ("paused"), fades the word out of view, replaces the faded word with a new word ("running"), then fades the new word into view. The net effect is that the status-indicating keyword within a sentence gracefully fades into a new word to alert the user of a change. This is a tremendously elegant effect that consists of only a few lines of simple code. If you were to perform this effect many times over a larger block of text, you could achieve an effect in which one message appears to sporadically change into another.

TRANSITIONING TEXT FANCIFULLY

You could easily swap the transition.fadeIn effect you've used thus far with another effect from Velocity's UI pack. Some of the other effects are quite fanciful, ranging from transition.shrinkIn, which causes an element to scale down into view, to transition.perspectiveDownIn, which causes an element to rotate down into view like a hinged barn door. (As always, the sophistication of your effects should be rooted in the principles discussed in Chapter 3, "Motion Design Theory.")

NOTE: For a complete list of UI pack effects, including live demos, visit VelocityJS.org/#uiPack.)

Keep in mind that some effects use 3D transforms (rotateX, rotateY, and translateZ), which don't work with on elements whose CSS display value is set to "inline"—the default display value for span and anchor elements in particular. The workaround is to set Blast's generated text elements to a display value of "inline-block", which keeps "inline" elements behaving as they normally do while giving them the added functionality of "block" elements (such as div and p), in which position-related properties, including 3D transforms, can be styled. Taking this display tweak into account, the inward text transition example would now look like this:

```
$("div")
  .html(message)
  .blast({ delimiter: "word" })
    .css({ opacity: 0, display: "inline-block" })
    .velocity("transition.perspectiveDownIn", { stagger: 50 });
```

This sets the Blasted text parts' display values to "inline-block" in the same call to jQuery's css() function that sets the elements' opacity to a starting value of 0.

TEXTUAL FLOURISHES

The final topic in this discussion of textual animation is the concept of *flourishes*, ambient animations that produce ongoing effects for aesthetic purposes. One example might be a string of text that flickers like a dying light bulb. Another might be having all the words in a sentence continuously animate to different shades of blue.

Both of these are bad ideas.

These effects distract users and ultimately amuse only you—the developer who enjoys toying with motion design. Never include animation just for the sake of animation; if a part of your page is meaninglessly drawing the user's attention away from the parts that have utility, go back to the drawing board.

The rare exception to this is status indicators—text such as "Loading..."—that keep the user abreast of what the interface is doing. These are appropriate targets for textual flourishes because the flourishes tell the user that the interface is still processing data (as opposed to having frozen). In this way, flourishes act as an engaging visual heartbeat.

So if textual flourishes are generally considered bad practice, why is this section even included in the book? Because flourishes *that aren't animated* are often a great idea! Consider this a non-animation bonus provided by Blast: you can stylize the text elements generated by Blast to produce colorful collages and other unique typographic designs. For example, you could break apart a website's slogan text ("Delivering happiness right to your door!") word by word to reduce the opacity of each successive word, thereby creating a subtle gradient effect that spans the entire sentence. Here's what that code would look like:

```
<div>
   Hi Mom
</div>
// Blast the div then iterate through the generated text elements
$("div").blast({ delimiter: "character" }).each(function(i, element) {
   // Successively reduce the opacity of each element with an
   → arbitrary formula
   var adjustedOpacity = 1 - i/10;
   element.style.opacity = adjustedOpacity;
});
```

Instead of iterating opacity values, you could also iterate RGB values to create color-based gradients. For example, if you increased the blue component of text whose color initially starts as gray, you'd produce elements that are increasingly rich in blue as you go from first to last:

```
// Blast the div then iterate through the generated text elements
$("div").blast({ delimiter: "character" }).each(function(i, element) {
    // Successively increase the blue color component of each element
    → with an arbitrary formula
    var adjustedBlue = i*20;
    element.style.opacity = "rgb(0, 0," + adjustedBlue + ")";
});
```

remember: form follows function.

WRAPPING UP

This is just the beginning of the possibilities created by granular text control. Other techniques include fine-tuning the coordinates of every letter in a word to produce a collage effect, or placing words around the circumference of a circle to mimic the typographic design you might find on a drink coaster.

While these techniques may be well-suited for bold homepage centerpieces, they may not be appropriate for critical parts of your UI that are subject to repeated user interaction. Why? Because stylized text is harder to read at a glance than unstylized text. But if you consider the balance between form and function, you'll be fine.

CHAPTER 6

Scalable Vector Graphics Primer

Since an in-depth tutorial on Scalable Vector Graphics (SVG) could easily comprise a book of its own, this chapter simply serves as an introduction to the topic. The goal is to equip you with enough knowledge to be comfortable animating SVG elements and to know where to go next to continue your learning.

CREATING IMAGES THROUGH CODE

An SVG element is a type of DOM element that borrows the syntax of the HTML elements you're already familiar with to define arbitrary shapes. SVG elements differ from HTML elements in that they have unique tags, attributes, and behaviors that allow them to define graphic shapes. Put another way, SVGs let you to create images through code. This is a tremendously powerful concept because it means you can programmatically style and animate these shapes using JavaScript and CSS. In addition SVG offers many other benefits:

- SVG compresses incredibly well. Graphics defined in SVG have smaller file sizes than their PNG/JPEG equivalents, which can greatly improve site load times.

- SVG graphics scale to any resolution without a loss of clarity. Unlike standard image formats, they look razor sharp across all devices—say good-bye to blurry images on mobile screens.

- Like HTML elements, SVG elements can be assigned event handlers that respond to a user's input, which means that the graphics on your page can be made interactive. If you so desired, all the buttons on your site could be turned into animated graphics.

- Many photo-editing apps (including Adobe Photoshop, Sketch, and Inkscape) let you export your design work into SVG format for quick copying and pasting into HTML. So, even if you don't consider yourself an artist, you can leverage third-party applications to do the designing for you.

In short, SVGs are an amazing graphics solution. Let's dive in!

SVG MARKUP

SVG elements are defined within a parent `<svg>` container. Specifying the width and height dimensions of container element defines the canvas that your SVG graphics render upon:

```
<svg version="1.1" width="500" height="500"
→ xmlns="http://www.w3.org/2000/svg">
  <circle cx="100" cy="100" r="30" />
  <rect id="rect" x="100" y="100" width="200" height="200" />
</svg>
```

Within `<svg>`, you can insert SVG shape elements of varying sorts. The above example has a `circle` element followed by a `rect` (rectangle) element. As with normal HTML elements, SVG elements accept `height` and `width` attributes, which are used here for demonstration purposes, but (as with HTML) it's considered best practice to specify SVG styling properties within a CSS stylesheet. Also as with HTML, stylesheet classes target SVG elements via their `id`, `class`, or tag types.

Where the SVG and HTML specifications fundamentally differ is in their range of accepted HTML attributes and CSS properties. SVG elements accept only a few of the standard CSS properties. Further, SVGs accept a special set of attributes, called *presentational attributes*, which include `fill`, `x`, and `y`. (`fill` specifies which color to fill a shape with, whereas `x` and `y` define the position of the element's top-left corner.) These attributes define how an element is visually rendered on its canvas. Let's run through a few of them, using `rect` as a sample SVG element:

```
<rect id="rect" x="100" y="100" width="200" height="200" />
```

Here, the width and height attributes work as you'd expect. The unique `x` and `y` attributes define the rectangle's coordinates within the canvas. These values simply position the rectangle relative to an `x = 0, y = 0` origin point. Unlike HTML, SVG positioning is not defined with `top`, `right`, `bottom`, `left`, `float`, or `margin` CSS properties; SVG positioning logic is fully dictated by explicitly defined coordinates. In other words, an SVG element's positioning doesn't affect the position of its sibling elements; instead of pushing each other around the page, SVG siblings simply overlap one another.

Now let's take a look at the `circle` element. Its rendering is specified via coordinates that designate its center point (cx and cy) along with a radius value (r) that designates its length:

```
<circle cx="100" cy="100" r="30" />
```

Pretty simple, right? SVG elements use the same markup structure as HTML elements, so all the code samples in this chapter should feel familiar.

Note that there are many other types of SVG elements, including *ellipse, line,* and *text.* See the end of this chapter for further details.

SVG STYLING

SVG elements accept a variety of special styling properties that are not available to HTML elements. SVG's `fill` property, for example, is similar to `background-color` in CSS, `stroke` is similar to `border-color`, and `stroke-width` is similar to `border-width`. Take a look at this example:

```
<svg version="1.1" width="500" height="500"
→ xmlns="http://www.w3.org/2000/svg">
  <circle cx="100" cy="100" r="30" style="fill: blue" />
  <rect id="rect" x="100" y="100" width="200" height="200"
  → style="fill: green; stroke: red; stroke-width: 5px" />
</svg>
```

Above, the `circle` element is filled with solid blue, and the `rect` element is filled with solid green. Additionally, the rectangle has a red border with a thickness of 5px.

There are many other SVG-specific styling properties. For now, it's simply important for you to know that they exist so you'll pay extra attention when trying to animate CSS properties on SVG elements.

NOTE: Refer to the "Wrapping up" section of this chapter for information on where to find a full listing of SVG styling properties.

SUPPORT FOR SVG

Out-of-the-box support for SVG element animation isn't great: neither jQuery nor CSS offers complete support for animating SVG-specific styling properties and presentational attributes. Further, CSS transitions can't animate SVG elements at all on Internet Explorer 9, and CSS can't be used to apply *transform* animations to SVG elements on any version of Internet Explorer.

To gain comprehensive SVG animation support, use either a dedicated SVG library or an animation library that has built-in support for SVG elements. One noteworthy dedicated SVG library is Snap.svg. It probably won't surprise you to learn that Velocity. js, the JavaScript animation library you've been using throughout this book, provides full support for SVG element animation.

NOTE: Go to SnapSVG.io to download the Snap.svg library.

SVG ANIMATION

SVG elements might never be the backbone of your UI, but they're certainly appropriate for spicing up the parts of your page that you'd normally fill with static images. Uses for SVGs include:

- Buttons with intricate animation sequences that are triggered when users hover and click.
- Unique loading status graphics that replace the all-too-common rotating indicator GIF.
- Company logos whose individual parts animate together upon page load.

   This last use case is explored in more detail later in this chapter.

PASSING IN PROPERTIES

With Velocity, SVG properties are animated in the same way that standard CSS properties are. Pass the appropriate properties and their desired end values into Velocity's properties object:

```
// Animate an SVG element to a red fill and a black stroke
$svgElement.velocity({ fill: "#ff0000", stroke: "#000000" });
```

In contrast, note that the code below would not work since the following CSS properties are not supported by SVG elements:

```
// Incorrect: These properties don't apply to SVG elements
$svgElement.velocity({ borderSize: "5px", borderColor: "#000000" });
```

PRESENTATIONAL ATTRIBUTES

The presentational attributes explored earlier in this chapter are also animated as expected:

```
// Animate the x and y coordinates of a rectangle
$("rect").velocity({ x: 100, y: 100 });
// Animate the cx and cy coordinates of a circle
$("circle").velocity({ cx: 100, cy: 100 });
// Animate the dimensions of a rectangle
$("rect").velocity({ width: 200, height: 200 });
// Animate the radius of a circle
$("circ").velocity({ r: 100 });
```

All the Velocity features that you're currently using—animation reversal, UI pack effects, sequence triggering, and so on—also work as expected with SVG elements.

POSITIONAL ATTRIBUTES VS. TRANSFORMS

You might be wondering what the difference is between using the x, cx, y, and cy positional attributes instead of CSS transforms (e.g. translateX, translateY) when specifying the positions of SVG elements. The answer is *browser support*. Internet Explorer (up to and including Internet Explorer 11) does not support CSS transforms on SVG elements. Consider the following:

```
// The x and y attributes work everywhere that SVG elements do
→ (IE8+, Android 3+)
$("rect").velocity({ x: 100, y: 100 });
// Alternatively, positional transforms (such as translateX and translateY)
→ work everywhere *except* Internet Explorer
$("rect").velocity({ translateX: 100, translateY: 100 });
```

NOTE: Although transforms are known to be particularly performant due to hardware acceleration (read more on this in Chapter 7, "Animation Performance"), both approaches to SVG animation are equally fast since SVG graphics are hardware-accelerated by default.

SVG lets you go beyond rectangles.

IMPLEMENTATION EXAMPLE: ANIMATED LOGOS

High-resolution site logos that animate into place upon page load are ideal targets for SVG implementation. Suppose you want to crudely replicate the MasterCard logo, which consists of two overlapping circles of different colors. If you were to animate this logo into place using Velocity, you'd start with an SVG canvas defined as follows:

```
<svg version="1.1" width="500" height="500"
→ xmlns="http://www.w3.org/2000/svg">
  <circle id="circleLeft" cx="100" cy="100" r="30" style="fill: red" />
  <circle id="circleRight" cx="100" cy="100" r="30"
    → style="fill: orange" />
</svg>
```

This creates two overlapping circles with identical radii. Next, you'd animate the circles outward from their origins so that they overlap only slightly when they're done animating:

```
// Move one circle toward the left
$("#circleLeft").velocity({ cx: "-=15px" }, { easing: "spring" });
// Move one circle toward the right
$("#circleRight").velocity({ cx: "+=15px" }, { easing: "spring" });
```

Here, the left circle is animated 15 pixels leftward (using the "-=" operator to instruct Velocity to decrement the circle's current value) and the right circle is animated 15 pixels rightward. The spring easing provides added flair by making the circles bounce away from one another with propulsive force.

Since SVG elements can listen for mouse-based events (clicks, hovers, and so on), you could improve upon this demo by turning it into an example of SVG element interaction. With the aid of jQuery and Velocity, one such implementation could look like this:

```
$("svg").on("mouseover mouseout", function() {
  $("#circleLeft, #circleRight").velocity("reverse");
});
```

This triggers a reversal of the circles' page-load animation when the user hovers on or off the SVG element. The single line of code accomplishes this by leveraging Velocity's reverse animation command. For more on working with reverse, refer to Chapter 2, "Animating with Velocity.js." In effect, when the user first hovers, the page-load animation is reversed. When the user then hovers off, the reversal is itself reversed, bringing the logo back to its original form.

While this code example is undoubtedly anticlimactic, this is once again a *good thing* because it reflects the similarities between animating SVG and HTML elements. Where SVGs do start to become uniquely complex is when you define arbitrary shapes that go beyond the basics of squares, rectangles, circles, and so on. After all, SVG elements can define any shape you can dream up in a photo editor, so they have to be tremendously expressive. And they are. But mastering SVG design is beyond the scope of this book. See the "Wrapping up" section of this chapter to learn where to go next to continue learning.

WRAPPING UP

If you're intrigued by what you've read so far and want to learn more about working with SVGs, check out these great resources:

- For a full overview of working with SVG elements, refer to Joni Trythall's fantastic and free SVG Pocket Guide (https://github.com/jonitrythall/svgpocketguide).

- For a directory of SVG element types and their properties, consult Mozilla Developer Network (https://developer.mozilla.org/en-US/docs/Web/SVG).

- For a listing of all the SVG attributes and styling properties that Velocity can animate, refer to VelocityJS.org/#svg.

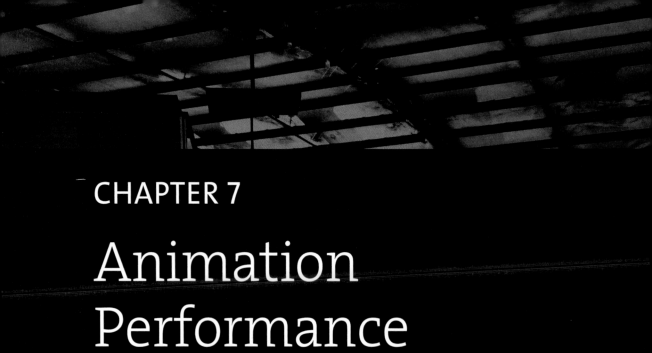

CHAPTER 7

Animation Performance

Performance affects everything. Increased performance—apparent or real—drastically improves UX, which in turn boosts your company's *bottom line.* Several major studies have demonstrated that latency increases on search engines result in significant decreases in revenue per user. To put it bluntly, *people hate waiting.*

As explained in Chapter 1, JavaScript animation performance is comparable to that of CSS animation. So, if you're using a modern animation library such as Velocity.js, the performance of your animation engine is not your app's bottleneck—it's your own code. That's what this chapter explores: techniques for coding high-performance animations across all browsers and devices.

THE REALITY OF WEB PERFORMANCE

If you've ever wondered why running concurrent animations slows down your UI, or why your site performs slowly on mobile devices, this chapter is for you.

Animations are a very resource-intensive process for browsers to perform, but there are many techniques that can help the browser work as efficiently as possible. We're about to learn them.

From the perspective of UI design, there's no shortage of articles extolling the virtues of building mobile-first, responsive websites. Conversely, from the perspective of UI *performance*, most of us, as developers, are unaware of what best practices are or how to follow them. Staying abreast of the web performance landscape is overwhelming and oftentimes futile; we're held captive by browser and device quirks, byproducts of the volume of devices (desktops, smartphones, and tablets) and browsers (Chrome, Android, Firefox, Safari, Internet Explorer) that crowd the ecosystem. Considering that these platforms are continuously updated, it's no surprise that we often throw in the towel and sideline performance concerns as much as we can. Sometimes we may even be tempted to do away with animations altogether if we're unsure how to implement them without sacrificing performance.

We tell ourselves:

> *Since devices are getting faster, as users continue upgrading their hardware, my site will become progressively more performant.*

Unfortunately, the global reality is the exact opposite: the smartphones that the developing world is adopting fall short of the performance of the latest iPhones in our pockets. Do you really want to forsake building products for the next *few billion* people coming online? The upcoming Firefox OS initiative is poised to bring capable smartphones to hundreds of millions of people, so we're not simply waxing poetic about hypotheticals. The mobile revolution is here *now*.

NOTE: Ericsson has reported that the global smartphone subscriber count will rise from 1.9 billion to 5.9 billion in the next five years— fueled almost exclusively by the developing world.

performance affects everything.

If your gut reaction is, "It's not my problem—my app is just for the tech-savvy middle-class in the developed world," rest assured that your evil web developer twin is sitting two thousand miles away cackling at the thought of getting to a nascent market before you do by actually putting in the effort necessary to deliver great experiences on low-powered devices. (There's actually an enormous conglomerate dedicated to this— search Google for "Rocket Internet.")

There's another nasty reality to sidelining performance concerns: we systematically make the mistake of testing our sites on devices operating under *ideal* loads. In reality, of course, users have multiple apps and browser tabs running concurrently. Their devices are working overtime to process a dozen tasks at any given time. Accordingly, the performance baseline established for your app probably doesn't reflect its performance in the real world. Yikes!

But, fear not, keen developer. It's time to explore the performance techniques at your disposal and level up your animation game.

TECHNIQUE: REMOVE LAYOUT THRASHING

Layout thrashing—the lack of synchronization in DOM manipulation—is the 800-pound gorilla in animation performance. There's no painless solution, but there are best practices. Let's explore.

PROBLEM

Consider how webpage manipulation consists of *setting* and *getting*: you can *set* (update) or *get* (query) an element's CSS properties. Likewise, you can insert new elements onto a page (a set) or you can query for a set of existing elements (a get). Gets and sets are the core browser processes that incur performance overhead (another is graphical rendering). Think of it this way: after setting new properties on an element, the browser has to calculate the resulting impacts of your changes. For example, changing the width of one element can trigger a chain reaction in which the width of the element's parent, siblings, and children elements must also change depending on their respective CSS properties.

The UI performance reduction that occurs from alternating sets with gets is called *layout thrashing*. While browsers are highly optimized for page-layout recalculations, the extent of their optimizations is greatly diminished by layout thrashing. Performing a series of gets at once, for example, can easily be optimized by the browser into a single, streamlined operation because the browser can cache the page's state after the first get, then reference that state for each subsequent get. However, repeatedly performing one get followed by one set forces the browser to do a lot of heavy lifting since its cache is continuously invalidated by the changes made by set.

This performance impact is exacerbated when layout thrashing occurs within an animation loop. Consider how an animation loop aims to achieve 60 frames per second, the threshold at which the human eye perceives buttery-smooth motion. What this means is that every tick in an animation loop must complete within 16.7ms (1 second/ 60 ticks ~= 16.67ms). Layout thrashing is a very easy way to cause each tick to exceed this limit. The end result, of course, is that your animation will stutter (or *jank*, in web animation parlance).

While some animation engines, such as Velocity.js, contain optimizations to reduce the occurrence of layout thrashing inside their own animation loops, be careful to avoid layout thrashing in your *own* loops, such as the code inside a setInterval() or a self-invoking setTimeout().

SOLUTION

Avoiding layout thrashing consists of simply batching together DOM sets and DOM gets. The following code causes layout thrashing:

```
// Bad practice
var currentTop = $("element").css("top"); // Get
$("element").style.top = currentTop + 1; // Set
var currentLeft = $("element").css("left"); // Get
$("element")..style.left = currentLeft + 1; // Set
```

If you rewrite the code so that all queries and updates are aligned, the browser can batch the respective actions and reduce the extent to which this code causes layout trashing:

```
var currentTop = $("element").css("top"); // Get
var currentLeft = $("element").css("left"); // Get
$("element").css("top", currentTop + 1); // Set
$("element").css("left", currentLeft + 1); // Set
```

The illustrated problem is commonly found in production code, particularly in situations where UI operations are performed depending on the current value of an element's CSS property.

Say your goal is to toggle the visibility of a side menu when a button is clicked. To accomplish this, you might first check to see if the side menu has its display property set to either "none" or "block", then you'd proceed to alternate the value as appropriate. The process of checking for the display property constitutes a get, and whichever action is subsequently taken to show or hide the side menu will constitute a set.

The optimized implementation of this code would entail maintaining a variable in memory that's updated whenever the button is clicked, and checking that variable for the side menu's current status before toggling its visibility. In this way, the get can be skipped altogether, which helps reduce the likelihood of the code producing a set alternated with a get. Further, beyond reducing the likelihood of layout thrashing, the UI now also benefits from having one less page query. Keep in mind that each set and get is a relatively expensive browser operation; the fewer there are, the faster your UI will perform.

Many tiny improvements ultimately add up to a substantial benefit, which is the underlying theme of this chapter: Follow as many performance best practices as you can, and you'll wind up with a UI that rarely sacrifices your desired motion design goals for the sake of performance.

JQUERY ELEMENT OBJECTS

Instantiating *jQuery element objects* (JEO) is the most common culprit of DOM gets. You may be wondering what a JEO is, but you've certainly seen this code snippet before:

```
$("#element").css("opacity", 1);
```
... or its raw JavaScript equivalent:
```
document.getElementById("element").style.opacity = 1;
```

In the case of the jQuery implementation, the value returned by `$("#element")` is a JEO, which is an object that wraps the raw DOM element that was queried. JEO's provide you with access to all of your beloved jQuery functions, including `.css()`, `.animate()`, and so on.

In the case of the raw JavaScript implementation, the value returned by `getElementById("element")` is the raw (unwrapped) DOM element. In both implementations, the browser is instructed to search through the DOM tree to find the desired element. This is an operation that, when repeated in bulk, impacts page performance.

This performance concern is exacerbated when *uncached* elements are used in code snippets that are repeated, such as the code contained by a loop. Consider the following example:

```
$elements.each(function(i, element) {
    $("body").append(element);
});
```

You can see how $("body") is a JEO instantiation that's repeated for every iteration of the $.each() loop: In addition to appending the loop's current element to the DOM (which has its own performance implications), you're now also repeatedly forcing a DOM query. Seemingly harmless one-line operations like these add up very quickly.

The solution here is to cache the results—or, save the returned JEO's into variables—to avoid a repeated DOM operation every time you want to call a jQuery function on an element. Hence, the code goes from looking like this:

```
// Bad practice: We haven't cached our JEO
$("#element").css("opacity", 1);
// ... some intermediary code...
// We instantiate the JEO again
$("#element").css("opacity", 0);
```

to looking like this after it's properly optimized:

```
// Cache the jQuery element object, prefixing the variable with $
→ to indicate a JEO
var $element = $("#element");
$element.css("opacity", 1);
// ... some intermediary code...
// We re-use the cached JEO and avoid a DOM query
$element.css("opacity", 0);
```

Now you can reuse $element throughout your code without ever incurring a repeated DOM lookup on its behalf.

FORCE-FEEDING

Traditionally, animation engines query the DOM at the start of an animation to determine the initial value of each CSS property being animated. Velocity offers a workaround to this page-querying event through a feature called *force-feeding*. It's an alternative technique for avoiding layout thrashing. With force-feeding, you explicitly define your animations' start values so that these upfront gets are eliminated.

Force-fed start values are passed in as the second item in an array that takes the place of a property's value in an animation properties map. The first item in the array is the standard end value that you're animating toward.

Consider the following two animation examples, both of which are triggered upon page load:

```
// Animate translateX to 500px from a start value of 0
$element.velocity({ translateX: [ 500, 0 ] });
// Animate opacity to 0 from a start value of 1
$element.velocity({ opacity: [ 0, 1 ]);
```

In the first example, you're passing translateX a force-fed start value of 0 since you know that the element has yet to be translated (since the page has just loaded). You're force-feeding in what you know (or want) the original property value to be. Further, in the second example, the element's current opacity is 1 because that's the default value for opacity and you haven't yet modified the element in any way. In short, with force-feeding, you can reduce the browser's workload in situations where you have an understanding of how elements are already styled.

> **NOTE:** Force-feed animation properties only when they're first used in an animation chain, not when they occur subsequently in the chain, since Velocity already does internal caching there:
> ```
> $element
>     // Optionally forcefeed here
>     .velocity({ translateX: [ 500, 0 ] })
>     // Do not forcefeed here; 500 is internally cached
>     .velocity({ translateX: 1000 });
> ```

Force-feeding is an invaluable feature for high-stress situations such as animating a large number of elements at once on a desktop browser or when dealing with low-powered mobile devices for which every page interaction incurs a noticeable delay.

However, for most real-world UI animation situations, force-feeding is an unnecessary optimization that makes your code less maintainable due to having to update the force-fed start values whenever you change the elements' values within CSS stylesheets.

> **NOTE:** Refer to Chapter 8, "Animation Demo," to walk through an application of force-feeding.

TECHNIQUE: BATCH DOM ADDITIONS

Like reducing layout thrashing, batching DOM additions is another performance technique to help avoid unoptimized interaction with the browser.

PROBLEM

You're not done with gets and sets just yet! A common page set is the insertion of new DOM elements at run-time. While there are many uses for adding new elements to a page, perhaps the most popular is infinite scrolling, which consists of elements continuously animating into view at the bottom of a page while the user scrolls downward.

As you learned in the previous section, browsers have to compute the composition of all affected elements whenever a new element is added. This is a relatively slow process. Hence, when DOM insertion is performed many times per second, the page is hit with a significant performance impact. Fortunately, when processing multiple elements, browsers can optimize page set performance if all elements are inserted at the same time. Unfortunately, we as developers often unintentionally forgo this optimization by separating our DOM insertions. Consider the following example of unoptimized DOM insertion code:

```
// Bad practice
var $body = $("body");
var $newElements = [ "<div>Div 1</div>", "<div>Div 2</div>",
→ "<div>Div 3</div>" ];
$newElements.each(function(i, element) {
   $(element).appendTo($body);
   // Other arbitrary code
});
```

This iterates through a set of element strings that are instantiated into jQuery element objects (without a performance drawback since you're not querying the DOM for each JEO). Each element is then inserted into the page using jQuery's appendTo().

Here's the problem: even if additional code exists after the appendTo() statement, the browser won't compress these DOM sets into a single insertion operation because it can't be certain that asynchronous code operating outside the loop won't alter the DOM's state between insertions. For example, imagine if you queried the DOM to find out how many elements exist on the page after each insertion:

```
// Bad practice
$newElements.each(function(i, element) {
   $(element).appendTo($body);
   // Output how many children the body element has
   console.log($body.children().size());
});
```

The browser couldn't possibly optimize the DOM insertions into a single operation because the code explicitly asks the browser to tell us the accurate number of elements that exist before the next loop begins. For the browser to return the correct count each time, it can't have batched all insertions upfront.

In conclusion, when you perform DOM element insertion inside a loop, each insertion happens independently of any others, resulting in a notable performance sacrifice.

SOLUTION

Instead of individually inserting new elements into the DOM, construct the full DOM element set in memory, then insert it via a single call to appendTo(). The optimized version of the code shown in the section above now looks like this:

```
// Optimized
var $body = $("body");
var $newElements = [ "<div>Div 1</div>", "<div>Div 2</div>",
→ "<div>Div 3</div>" ];
var html = "";
$newElements.each(function(i, element) {
   html += element;
});
$(html).appendTo($body);
```

This concatenates the string representation of each HTML element onto a master string that is then turned into a JEO and appended into the DOM in a single shot. In this way, the browser is given explicit instruction to insert everything at once, and it optimizes for performance accordingly.

Simple, right? As you'll see in the remainder of this chapter, performance best practices are usually as easy as this. You simply have to train your eye to know when to use them.

the onus is on you.

TECHNIQUE: AVOID AFFECTING NEIGHBORING ELEMENTS

It's important to consider the impact of an element's animation on neighboring elements.

PROBLEM

When an element's dimensions are animated, the changes often affect the positioning of nearby elements. For example, if an element between two sibling elements shrinks in width, the siblings' absolute positions will dynamically change so they remain next to the animating element. Another example might be animating a child element nested inside a parent element that doesn't have explicitly defined width and height properties. Accordingly, when the child is being animated, the parent will also resize itself so that it continues to fully wrap itself around the child. In effect, the child element is no longer the only element being animated—the parent's dimensions are also being animated, and that's even more work for the browser to perform upon each tick in an animation loop!

There are many CSS properties whose modification can result in dimensional and positional adjustments to neighboring elements, including top, right, bottom, and left; all margin and padding properties; border thickness; and the width and height dimensions.

As a performance-minded developer, you need to appreciate the impact that animating these properties can have on your page. Always ask yourself how each property you're attempting to animate affects nearby elements. If there's a way to rewrite your code such that you can isolate elements' changes from one another, then consider doing so. In fact, there *is* an easy way to do just this—on to the solution!

SOLUTION

The simple solution to avoid affecting neighboring elements is to animate the CSS *transform* properties (translateX, translateY, scaleX, scaleY, rotateZ, rotateX, and rotateY) whenever possible. The *transform* properties are unique in that they elevate targeted elements to isolated layers that are rendered separately from the rest of the page (with a performance boost courtesy of your GPU), so that neighboring elements aren't affected. For example, when animating an element's translateX to a value of "500px", the element will move 500px rightward while superimposing itself on top of whatever elements exist along its animation path. If there are no elements along its path (that is, if there are no nearby elements for it to affect), then using translateX will have the same net effect on the look of your page as if you had animated using the much slower left property.

Hence, whenever possible, an animation that once looked like this:

```
// Move the element 500px from the left
$element.velocity({ left: "500px" });
```

should be refactored into this:

```
// Faster: Use translateX
$element.velocity({ translateX: "500px" });
```

Similarly, if you can substitute translateY for top, do so:

```
$element.velocity({ top: "100px" });
// Faster: Use translateY
$element.velocity({ translateY: "100px" });
```

> **NOTE:** Sometimes you actually intend to use left or top so that neighboring elements' positions are changed. In all other cases, get into the habit of using the transform properties. The performance impact is significant.

CONSIDER OPACITY OVER COLOR

opacity is another CSS property that receives a GPU rendering boost since it doesn't affect the positioning of elements. So, if there are elements on your page for which you're currently animating, say, color when the user hovers over them, consider animating *opacity* instead. If the net effect looks almost as good as the color animation, then consider sticking with it—you've just boosted the UI's performance without compromising its look.

As a performance-minded developer, you're no longer allowed to arbitrarily select animation properties. You must now consider the impact of each of your property choices.

NOTE: Refer to CSSTriggers.com for a breakdown of how CSS properties affect browser performance.

TECHNIQUE: REDUCE CONCURRENT LOAD

Browsers have bottlenecks. Find out what they are and stay below them.

PROBLEM

When a page first loads, the browser processes HTML, CSS, JavaScript, and images as quickly as possible. It should come as no surprise that animations occurring during this time tend to be laggy—they're fighting for the browser's limited resources. So, despite the fact that a page's loading sequence is often a great time to flaunt all your motion design skills, it's best to restrain yourself if you want to avoid giving users the first impression that your site is laggy.

A similar concurrency bottleneck arises when many animations occur at once on a page—regardless of where they take place in the page's lifecycle. In these situations, browsers can choke under the stress of processing many styling changes at once, and stuttering can occur.

Fortunately, there are some clever techniques for reducing concurrent animation load.

SOLUTION

There are two approaches for addressing the concurrency issue: staggering and breaking up animations into sequences.

STAGGER

One way to reduce concurrent animation load is to make use of Velocity's UI pack's stagger feature, which delays the start times of successive animations in a set of elements by a specified duration. For example, to animate every element in a set toward an opacity value of 1 with successive 300ms delays between start times, your code might look like this:

```
$elements.velocity({ opacity: 1 }, { stagger: 300 });
```

The elements are no longer animating in perfect synchronization; instead, at the very start of the entire animation sequence, only the first element is animating. Later, at the very end of the entire sequence, only the last element is animating. You're effectively spreading out the animation sequence's total workload so that the browser is always performing less work at one time than it would have had it been animating every element simultaneously. What's more, implementing staggering into your motion design is often a good aesthetic choice. (Chapter 3, "Motion Design Theory," further explores the merits of staggering.)

MULTI-ANIMATION SEQUENCES

There's one more clever way to reduce concurrent load: break up property animations into multi-animation sequences. Take, for example, the case of animating an element's *opacity* value. This is typically a relatively low-stress operation. But, if you were to simultaneously animate the element's width and box-shadow properties, you'd be giving the browser appreciably more work to perform: more pixels will be affected, and more computation would be required.

Hence, an animation that looks like this:

```
$images.velocity({ opacity: 1, boxShadowBlur: "50px" });
```

might be refactored into this:

```
$images
  .velocity({ opacity: 1 })
  .velocity({ boxShadowBlur: "50px" });
```

The browser has less concurrent work to do since these individual property animations occur one after another. Note that the creative tradeoff being made here is that we've opted to prolong the total animation sequence duration, which may or may not be desirable for your particular use case.

Since an optimization such as this entails changing the intention of your motion design, this is not a technique that should always be employed. Consider it a last resort. If you need to squeeze additional performance out of low-powered devices, then this technique may be suitable. Otherwise, don't pre-optimize the code on your site using techniques like this, or you'll end up with unnecessarily bloated and inexpressive code.

TECHNIQUE: DON'T CONTINUOUSLY REACT TO SCROLL AND RESIZE EVENTS

Be mindful of how often your code is being run. A fast snippet of code being run 1,000 times per second may—in aggregate—no longer be very fast.

PROBLEM

Browsers' scroll and resize events are two event types that are triggered at very high rates: when a user resizes or scrolls the browser window, the browser fires the callback functions associated with these events many times per second. Hence, if you've registered callbacks that interact with the DOM—or worse, contain layout thrashing— they can cause tremendously high browser load during times of scrolling and resizing. Consider the following code:

```
// Perform an action when the browser window is scrolled
$(window).scroll(function() {
    // Anything in here is fired multiple times per second while the
    →  user scrolls
});
// Perform an action when the browser window is resized
$(window).resize(function() {
    // Anything in here is fired multiple times per second while the
    →  user resizes
});
```

Recognize that the functions above aren't simply called once when their respective events start; instead, they are called throughout the duration of the user's respective interaction with the page.

SOLUTION

The solution to this problem is to *debounce* event handlers. Debouncing is the process of defining an interval during which an event handler callback will be called only once. For example, say you defined a debounce interval of 250ms and the user scrolled the page for a total duration of 1000ms. The debounced event handler code would accordingly fire only four times (1000ms/250ms).

The code for a debounce implementation is beyond the scope of this book. Fortunately, many libraries exist exclusively to solve this problem. Visit davidwalsh.name/javascript-debounce-function for one example. Further, the tremendously popular Underscore.js (UnderscoreJS.org), a JavaScript library akin to jQuery that provides helper functions for making coding easier, includes a debounce function that you can easily reuse across your event handlers.

NOTE: As of this book's writing, the latest version of Chrome automatically debounces scroll events.

TECHNIQUE: REDUCE IMAGE RENDERING

Not all elements are rendered equally. Browsers have to work overtime when displaying certain elements. Let's look at which those are.

PROBLEM

Videos and images are multimedia element types that browsers have to work extra hard to render. Whereas the dimensional properties of non-multimedia HTML elements can be computed with ease, multimedia elements contain thousands of pixel-by-pixel data points that are computationally expensive for browsers to resize, reposition, and recomposite. Animating these elements will *always* be less less than optimal versus animating standard HTML elements such as div, p, and table.

Further, given that *scrolling* a page is nearly equivalent to *animating* a page (think of scrolling as animating the page's top property), multimedia elements can also drastically reduce scrolling performance on CPU-constrained mobile devices.

SOLUTION

Unfortunately, there's no way to "refactor" multimedia content into faster element types, other than turning simple, shape-based images into SVG elements wherever possible. Accordingly, the only available performance optimization is reducing the total number of multimedia elements that are displayed on the page at once and animated at once. Note that the words *at once* stress a reality of browser rendering: browsers only render what's visible. The portions of your page (including the portions that contain additional images) that *aren't* visible do not get rendered, and do not impose additional stress on browser processes.

So, there are two best practices to follow. First, if you're ever on the fence about adding an additional image to your page, opt to not include it. The fewer images there are to render, the better UI performance will be. (Not to mention the positive impact fewer images will have on your page's network load time.)

Second, if your UI is loading many images into view at once (say, eight or more, depending on your device's hardware capabilities), consider *not* animating the images at all, and instead crudely toggling the visibility of each image from invisible to visible. To help counteract how inelegant this can look, consider staggering visibility toggling so that the images load into view one after another instead of simultaneously. This will help guide the user's eye across the loading sequence, and will generally deliver more refined motion design.

NOTE: Refer to Chapter 3, "Motion Design Theory," to learn more about animation design best practices.

SNEAKY IMAGES

You're not done yet. There's more to this section than meets the eye, as we haven't fully explored the ways in which images can materialize on a page. The obvious culprit is the img element, but there are two other ways that images can sneak onto your pages.

CSS GRADIENTS

These are actually a type of image. Instead of being pre-produced by a photo editor, they are produced at run-time according to CSS styling definitions, for example, using a linear-gradient() as the background-image value on an element. The solution here is to opt for solid-color backgrounds instead of gradients whenever possible. Browsers can easily optimize the rendering of solid chunks of color, but, as with images, they have to work overtime to render gradients, which differ in color from pixel to pixel.

SHADOW PROPERTIES

The evil twin siblings of gradients are the box-shadow and text-shadow CSS properties. These are rendered similarly to gradients, but instead of stylizing background-color, they effectively stylize border-color. What's worse, they have opacity falloffs that require browsers to perform extra compositing work because the semitransparent portions of the gradients must be rendered against the elements underneath the animating element. The solution here is similar to the previous one: if your UI looks almost as good when you remove these CSS properties from your stylesheet, pat yourself on the back and never look back. Your website's performance will thank you.

These recommendations are simply that: *recommendations*. They are not performance best practices since they sacrifice your design intentions for increased performance. Considered them only as last resorts when your site's performance is poor and you've exhausted all other options.

TECHNIQUE: DEGRADE ANIMATIONS ON OLDER BROWSERS

You don't have to neglect supporting underperforming browsers and devices. If you embrace a performance-minded workflow from day one, you can simply provide them with a degraded—but completely functional—experience.

PROBLEM

Internet Explorer 8—a slow, outdated browser—is dying in popularity. But Internet Explorer 9, its successor, is still widely used outside of the Americas. Further, older Android smartphones running Android 2.3.x and below, which are slow relative to the latest-generation Android and iOS devices, also remain tremendously popular. Out of every ten users to your site, expect up to three of them to fall into one of these two groups (depending on the type of users your app attracts). Accordingly, if your site is rich in animation and other UI interactions, assume it will perform especially poorly for up to a third of your users.

SOLUTION

There are two approaches to addressing the performance issue raised by weaker devices: either broadly reduce the occurrence of animations across your entire site, or reduce them exclusively for the weaker devices. The former is a ultimately a product decision, but the latter is a simple technical decision that is easily implemented if you're using the global animation multiplier technique (or Velocity's equivalent *mock* feature) explained in the Chapter 4, "Animation Workflow." The global multiplier technique lets you dynamically alter the timing of animations across your entire site by setting a single variable. The trick then—whenever a weak browser is detected—is to set the multiplier to 0 (or set $.Velocity.mock to true) so that all of a page's animations complete within a single animation tick (less than 16ms):

```
// Cause all animations to complete immediately
$.Velocity.mock = true;
```

The result of this technique is that weaker devices experience UI animations that degrade so that instant style changes replace your animated transition. The benefits are significant: your UI will perform noticeably more smoothly without resource-intensive animations occurring on your page. While this technique is undoubtedly destructive (it compromises your motion design intentions), an improvement in usability is *always* worth a reduction in elegance. After all, users visit your app to accomplish specific goals, not to admire how clever your UI work is. Never let animations get in the way of user intentions.

If you're still irked by the notion of stripping animations from your UI, keep in mind that users on weaker devices are accustomed to websites behaving slowly for them. So, if your site bucks the trend in a constructive way, they'll be especially delighted by it and will be more likely to continue using it.

FIND YOUR PERFORMANCE THRESHOLD EARLY ON

Continuing from the previous technique's theme, it's worth stressing that the advice in this chapter is especially relevant for mobile devices, many of which are slow relative to desktop computers. Unfortunately, we, as developers, often fail to consider this in our workflows: we routinely create websites within the pristine operating environments of our high-end desktops, which are likely running the latest-generation hardware and software available. This type of environment is divorced from the real-world environments of users, who are often not only using outdated hardware and software, but tend to have many apps and browser tabs running simultaneously. In other words, most of us work in development environments that are non-representationally high-performance! The side effect of this oversight is that your app may actually be noticeably laggy for a significant portion of your users. By the time you asking what frustrates them, they may have already lost interest in using it.

The correct approach for a performance-minded developer is to determine the performance threshold early on in the development cycle. While developing your app, check its performance frequently on reference devices, which might include a last-generation mobile device plus a virtual machine running Internet Explorer 9. If you set a performance goal early on of being performant on your reference devices, then you can sleep soundly knowing that all newer devices will deliver even better performance for your users.

> **TIP:** If you're a Mac user, visit Microsoft's Modern.ie website for information on how to run free virtual copies of old Internet Explorer versions.

If you find that a reference device is too weak to power the motion design that you insist your app has, follow the advice from the previous technique: gracefully degrade animations on that reference device, and choose a faster device as your new (non-degraded) reference.

For each testing device, remember to open several apps and tabs at once so you simulate users' operating environments. Never test in a vacuum in which the only app running is your own.

Keep in mind that remote browser testing (through services such as BrowserStack. com and SauceLabs.com) is not the same as live reference device testing. Remote testing services are appropriate for testing for bugs and UI responsiveness—not for animation performance. After all, the test devices running in the cloud aren't using *real* hardware—they're emulated versions of devices. Consequently, their performance is typically different than that of their real-world counterparts. Further, the lag time between what occurs on the virtual machine and what's displayed on your browser window is too significant to get a meaningful gauge of UI animation performance.

In short, you'll need to go out and buy real devices for performance testing. Even if you're a cash-strapped developer, don't skimp on this. The few hundred dollars you spend on test devices will be offset by the increased recurring revenue you'll generate from happier users engaging more frequently with your buttery-smooth app.

If you wind up with a handful of reference devices, also consider purchasing Device Lab, a versatile stand that props up all of your mobile devices on a single surface so you can easily eyeball the screens during testing. As a bonus, the device includes a nifty app that lets you control all the browsers across your devices at once so you don't have to manually refresh each browser tab.

NOTE: Visit Vanamco.com to purchase and download Device Lab.

find your threshold early.

VISIT EBAY TO BUY OLD DEVICES FOR CHEAP

Purchasing the most popular Android and iOS devices from each of these products' major release cycles will give you a broad cross-section of the hardware and software environments that your users have. Here's my recommended setup (as of early 2015):

- iPhone 4 or iPad 2 running iOS7

- iPhone 5s (or newer) running the latest version of iOS

- Motorola Droid X running Android 2.3.x

- Samsung Galaxy SII running Android 4.1.x

- Samsung Galaxy S5 (or newer) running the latest version of Android

You're welcome to substitute any of the Android devices for devices of similar performance. What's important here is that you're using one device from each major Android release cycle (2.3.x, 4.1.x, and so on) so that you have a representative sample of the web browser performance from each one. Refer to http://developer.android.com/about/dashboards for a distribution of the most popular Android versions.

WRAPPING UP

Performance affects everything. From how many devices can run your app, to the quality of the user experience, to the perception of your app's technical competency, performance is a major tenet of professional web design. It's not a "nice-to-have," it's a fundamental building block. Don't relegate performance as a simple optimization to be made in hindsight.

CHAPTER 8

Animation Demo

It's time to get your hands dirty! This final chapter walks you through a full animation demo powered by Velocity. In going through the demo's source, you'll learn how Velocity's core features complement one another to greatly improve UI animation workflow. This demo will also introduce you to advanced techniques for working with CSS's transform properties, which are vital to web-based animation today.

In short, you're going to put together the skills you've accumulated throughout this book to make something really darn cool. Your goals in coding the demo are twofold: use terse and expressive animation code, and ensure maximum performance.

BEHAVIOR

The demo consists of 250 circles floating in, out, and around the screen. Periodically, you'll zoom in, then back out to the position where the virtual camera started. The first image presented momentarily shows a zoomed-in view.

NOTE: Before you continue reading, head on over to VelocityJS.org/demo.book.html to see a live preview of the demo. (You can right-click anywhere on the page then choose "View Source" to see the demo's code.)

The circle elements are simply normal `div`s with `box-shadow` and `border-radius` set in CSS. There's no WebGL or Canvas animation going on here—just pure HTML element manipulation. (Given the volume of elements that are being animated at once, it's quite impressive that this demo is capable of running so smoothly in the DOM!)

Let's break down the animation: It consists of `div` elements translating along the X, Y, and Z axes. The Z-axis dictates the depth of each element's animation, whereas X and Y provide the general flowing, 2D movement seen across the screen. Concurrent to the elements' individual movements is a larger perspective shift that occurs on the element containing all these `div`s. This perspective shift occurs every 3 seconds, and it creates a periodic zooming effect that makes the viewer feel as if he's briefly traveling through the circles' 3D space.

The second graphic depicts the 3D scene in its zoomed-out view. Contrast this with the zoomed-in view shown in the first image.

HOW TO DOWNLOAD THE CODE SAMPLE

The code behind this animation demo is available for download from peachpit.com. Here's how to get it:

1. Go to www.peachpit.com/register and create or log in to your account.

2. Enter the book's ISBN (978-0-13-409670-4) and click Submit.

3. Your "My Registered Products" page opens. Find the listing for this book, and click "Access Bonus Content."

4. The page containing the download link opens—click to access the Animation Demo file entitled *WebAnimationJS_DemoCodeSample.zip*

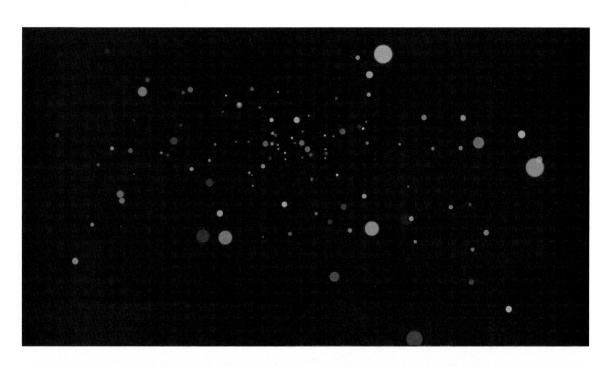

CODE STRUCTURE

Let's take a look at the code that powers this demo. It is structured as follows:

5. **Animation setup:** The specification of parameters used for constraining animation movement.

6. **Circle creation:** The generation of the div elements to be animated.

7. **Container animation:** The code responsible for animating the circles' parent element.

8. **Circle animation:** The code responsible for animating the circle elements themselves.

Try to familiarize yourself with the broader strokes of the demo's implementation so you can keep its full context in mind as you explore each individual code block in the upcoming sections:

```
/***********************
    Animation setup
***********************/
/* Randomly generate an integer between two numbers. */
function r (min, max) {
 return Math.floor(Math.random() * (max - min + 1)) + min;
}
/* Query the window's dimensions. */
var screenWidth = window.screen.availWidth,
   screenHeight = window.screen.availHeight;
/* Define the z-axis animation range. */
var translateZMin = -725,
   translateZMax = 600;
```

```
/*********************
    Circle creation
*********************/
var circleCount = 250,
   circlesHtml = "",
   $circles = "";
for (var i = 0; i < circleCount; i++) {
   circlesHtml += "<div class='circle'></div>";
}
$circle = $(circlesHtml);


/*****************************
     Container animation
*****************************/
$container
   .css("perspective-origin", screenWidth/2 + "px " +
   → screenHeight/2 + "px")
   .velocity(
   {
     perspective: [ 215, 50 ],
     opacity: [ 0.90, 0.55 ]
   }, {
     duration: 800,
     loop: 1,
     delay: 3000
   });
```

```
/***************************
      Circle animation
***************************/
$circles
  .appendTo($container)
  .velocity({
    opacity: [
      function() { return Math.random() },
      function() { return Math.random() + 0.1 }
    ],
    translateX: [
      function() { return "+=" + r(-screenWidth/2.5, screenWidth/2.5) },
      function() { return r(0, screenWidth) }
    ],
    translateY: [
      function() { return "+=" + r(-screenHeight/2.75,
        → screenHeight/2.75) },
      function() { return r(0, screenHeight) }
    ],
    translateZ: [
      function() { return "+=" + r(translateZMin, translateZMax) },
      function() { return r(translateZMin, translateZMax) }
    ]
  }, { duration: 6000 })
  .velocity("reverse", { easing: "easeOutQuad" })
  .velocity({ opacity: 0 }, 2000);
```

CODE SECTION: ANIMATION SETUP

This section's code is copied below for easy reference:

```
/***********************
    Animation setup
***********************/
/* Randomly generate an integer between two numbers. */
function r (min, max) {
  return Math.floor(Math.random() * (max - min + 1)) + min;
}
/* Query the window's dimensions. */
var screenWidth = window.screen.availWidth,
    screenHeight = window.screen.availHeight;
/* Define the z-axis animation range. */
var translateZMin = -725,
    translateZMax = 600;
```

The first section, Animation setup, begins by defining a function r (abbreviated from "random") that lets you artificially constrain randomly generated integer values. This function takes min and max parameters, then outputs a random number between the min to max range (using some basic algebra). You'll use this later when randomizing the animating elements' CSS transform values within ranges that are predefined in the next two code blocks.

The next section queries the window object to retrieve the monitor's dimensions. By later referencing these values, you can ensure that the circles don't animate too far off-screen (and consequently out of view).

Animation setup concludes by defining the `min` and `max` values for the elements' Z-axis movement. These values control how small (far away) or large (nearby) you want the circles to animate from their initial size. Specifically, it dictates that the circles can go as far as 725 pixels along the Z-axis away from the virtual camera (away from the screen), and as close as 600 pixels toward the camera. In this case, there's no constraint of going off-screen, but the circle could become too distant to see or so close that it takes up the entire monitor. Basically, it's a creative decision.

CODE SECTION: CIRCLE CREATION

```
/*********************
    Circle creation
*********************/
var circleCount = 250,
    circlesHtml = "",
    $circles = "";
for (var i = 0; i < circleCount; i++) {
    circlesHtml += "<div class='circle'></div>";
}
$circle = $(circlesHtml);
```

The demo's second section, Circle creation, generates the primary div elements to be animated. Here, it first defines the desired number of circles as `circleCount`. Then, it defines a `circlesHtml` string to contain the circles' collated HTML.

Next, it iterates up to the `circleCount` number to generate the circles' HTML. Notice that it uses the performance best practice of *batching DOM additions*, as detailed in Chapter 7, "Animation Performance." It collates the markup for each `div` element onto a master `circlesHtml` string that's later inserted into the DOM in a single action. (If you were to insert the `div` elements into the DOM one at a time, the negative performance impact would be significant: UI interaction in the browser would be frozen until the relatively slow element insertion process completed.)

Finally, it wraps the circle elements in a jQuery element object so they can be easily manipulated as a group in the upcoming Circle animation section.

CODE SECTION: CONTAINER ANIMATION

```
/*****************************
      Container animation
*****************************/
$container
  .css("perspective-origin", screenWidth/2 + "px " +
  → screenHeight/2 + "px")
  .velocity(
  {
      perspective: [ 215, 50 ],
      opacity: [ 0.90, 0.55 ]
  }, {
      duration: 800,
      loop: 1,
      delay: 3000
  });
```

3D CSS PRIMER

Let's begin the first of the two animation sections of the codebase by focusing on the element that contains the circle elements. Before diving into the code, however, here's a primer on how 3D animation works in the browser:

In order for 3D transforms to work (for example, translateZ, rotateX, rotateY), the CSS specification requires that the perspective CSS property be set on the element's parent. In this case, that's what the $container element is for.

The greater the value that perspective is set to, the less distance Z-axis translations (via CSS's translateZ) appear to move relative to their origin. In other words, if you want more exaggerated depth in your 3D animations, set the parent element's perspective property to something low, such as 50px, which is in fact the value that the container element is set to in the demo's CSS. In contrast, a higher perspective value, such as 250px, would result in less visible movement from the origin point for every pixel that the element's translateZ property is incremented by.

A separate and complementary CSS property is `prospective-origin`, which defines the angle at which the virtual camera is positioned. The virtual camera is the peephole through which the viewer sees 3D animation unfold in the browser. This section's code block uses jQuery's `$.css()` function to set a `perspective-origin` value on the container element that results in the camera being positioned at the center of the page, creating a perpendicular view of the 3D animation. This perpendicular view results in the appearance of circles flying directly toward and away from the viewer.

Specifically, this code section sets `perspective-origin` to the point on the page that's at half the browser's height and half its width—the center point of the page. This leverages the *window* dimensions queried in the Animation setup section.

With that context out of the way, let's explore this section's code.

PROPERTIES

This section's code, reproduced below for easy reference, creates the demo's zooming in and out effect:

```
$container
  .css("perspective-origin", screenWidth/2 + "px " +
  → screenHeight/2 + "px")
  .velocity(
  {
    perspective: [ 215, 50 ],
    opacity: [ 0.90, 0.55 ]
  }, {
    duration: 800,
    loop: 1,
    delay: 3250
  });
```

While the `prospective-origin` property is set once on the container element and thereafter left alone, the `prospective` property is being animated by Velocity. This is necessary because the intended effect of the demo is to keep the vantage point into the scene stationary (perpendicular), but to exaggerate then de-exaggerate the distance of the elements from the virtual camera, which is where the `perspective` property's animation comes in.

Specifically, this section uses Velocity to animate the `perspective` CSS property to a final value of 215px from a starting value of 50px.

By passing in an array as an animation property's value, you're forcefully specifying the final value to animate the property *toward* (215px, in the case above) as well as the initial value to animate *from* (50px, in the case above). While you certainly could have passed the property a single integer value as is typically expected by Velocity, the force-feeding syntax provides increased control over the property's complete animation path.

You might be wondering, isn't force-feeding unnecessary since Velocity knows how to retrieve a CSS property's starting value on its own? While that is Velocity's standard behavior when an integer is passed in as a value instead of an array, this isn't always a desirable behavior due to the performance drawbacks inherent to querying the DOM for a property's starting value. What the force-feeding syntax allows you to do is explicitly pass in a starting value so that Velocity can avoid querying the DOM for a property whose starting value you already know. In other words, the 50px starting value used in the `perspective` code above is the same value you initially set the container element's `perspective` property to in the CSS stylesheet. You're simply repeating the value here. Notice that this same force-feeding technique is used on the element's `opacity` property as well: it's animated to a final value of 0.90 from a starting value of 0.55 since that's what the property was set to in the CSS.

As discussed thoroughly in Chapter 7, "Animation Performance," DOM queries are indeed the Achilles' heel of performant animation: the browser performs resource-intensive calculations to determine the visual state of an element. While it's not important to the demo's performance that you include this performance optimization, since the associated Velocity animation isn't being triggered repeatedly inside a loop, it's included nonetheless to contrast force-feeding's secondary use, which you'll learn about later in this chapter.

The net effect of animating the `perspective` and `opacity` is that all of the container's circle elements appear to zoom in closer to the virtual camera while animating to an increased brightness (`opacity` goes from 0.55 to 0.90). The opacity boost mimics the way that light behaves in the real world: the closer the viewer is to the objects, the brighter they appear!

OPTIONS

The final section of Container animation code includes the options being passed into Velocity: `duration`, which is self explanatory; `delay`, which inserts a time-out at the start of the animation, and `loop`, which loops an animation back and forth between the values defined in the properties map and the element's values prior to the animation occurring. Specifically, by setting `loop` to 2, you're telling Velocity to animate to the values in properties map, back to where they were before, then to repeat this full loop iteration once more after a 3000ms delay.

> **NOTE:** When `delay` is set alongside `loop`, the delay occurs between each of the loop's alternations. Using delay creates a pleasant pause so that the zoom-in and zoom-out effect doesn't zigzag back and forth abruptly.

CODE SECTION: CIRCLE ANIMATION

This is where things start getting interesting. Let's take a look the circle animation, in which you're simultaneously animating their X-, Y-, Z-axis translations individually. You're also animating their opacity.

```
/***************************
    Circle animation
***************************/
$circles
  .appendTo($container)
  .velocity({
    opacity: [
      function() { return Math.random() },
      function() { return Math.random() + 0.1 }
    ],
    translateX: [
      function() { return "+=" + r(-screenWidth/2.5, screenWidth/2.5) },
      function() { return r(0, screenWidth) }
    ],
    translateY: [
      function() { return "+=" + r(-screenHeight/2.75,
        → screenHeight/2.75) },
      function() { return r(0, screenHeight) }
    ],
    translateZ: [
      function() { return "+=" + r(translateZMin, translateZMax) },
      function() { return r(translateZMin, translateZMax) }
    ]
  }, { duration: 6000 })
  .velocity("reverse", { easing: "easeOutQuad" })
  .velocity({ opacity: 0 }, 2000);
```

VALUE FUNCTIONS

Unlike the static animation property values used in the previous section (for example, [215, 50]), this section uses *functions* for property values: each property is force-fed an array of start and end values that are dynamically produced by functions. Let's briefly explore these *value functions*, which are a unique feature of Velocity.

NOTE: Read more about value functions at VelocityJS.org/#valueFunctions.

Value functions let you pass in functions as animation property values. These functions trigger at run-time, and are called individually for each element animated in a set. In the demo, the set in question is the circle divs contained within the $circles jQuery element object. Consequently, each circle element property will be assigned its own randomized value once the animation begins. The only other way to achieve differentiation between animation properties in a set of elements is to animate the elements separately by looping through them, which gets messy and performs badly. This is the benefit of value functions—you keep dynamic animation code terse and maintainable.

Notice that, to produce the randomized values, this section of code leverages our r helper function that was defined in Animation setup. (As a reminder, the r function returns a randomized integer value constrained by its min and max arguments.) You'll learn more about this function momentarily.

OPACITY ANIMATION

The opacity property animates from and toward randomized values. In the case of the starting value, you're giving the randomized value a slight boost to ensure that the elements are never too close to being invisible—after all, you want the viewer to see what you're animating! The animation of opacity results in a smattering of circles all over the page that have varying opacities from the very first frame. Differentiated opacities create a nice gradient effect that adds visual richness to the demo.

This code takes advantage of force-feeding for a purpose other than performance optimization: value functions are being force-fed to dynamically generate start values for the elements that have yet to be inserted into the DOM, which means that you're successfully avoiding writing an entirely new code block just to set the initial CSS states of the circle elements. You're dynamically providing unique starting positions in the same line of code responsible for animating those positions. As discussed thoroughly in Chapter 4, "Animation Workflow," you should strive for this level of expressiveness in all of your animation code.

TRANSLATION ANIMATION

For easy reference, here's this section's code once again:

```
/***************************
    Circle animation
***************************/
$circles
    .appendTo($container)
    .velocity({
      opacity: [
        function() { return Math.random() },
        function() { return Math.random() + 0.1 }
      ],
      translateX: [
        function() { return "+=" + r(-screenWidth/2.5, screenWidth/2.5) },
        function() { return r(0, screenWidth) }
      ],
      translateY: [
        function() { return "+=" + r(-screenHeight/2.75,
        → screenHeight/2.75) },
        function() { return r(0, screenHeight) }
      ],
      translateZ: [
        function() { return "+=" + r(translateZMin, translateZMax) },
        function() { return r(translateZMin, translateZMax) }
      ]
    }, { duration: 6000 })
    .velocity("reverse", { easing: "easeOutQuad" })
    .velocity({ opacity: 0 }, 2000);
```

It's time to examine the `translate` animations, which individually translate the circle elements' positions within the demo's 3D space. All three axes are animating from a randomized start value toward a randomized end value. The value operator, which consists of the plus sign followed by the equals sign (+=), tells the animation engine to animate properties incrementally from their starting values. In other words, the += value operator instructs the animation engine to treat the ending value as a relative value. In contrast, the default behavior of an animation engine is to interpret an end value in absolute terms.

As with `opacity`, this code section leverages force-feeding and value functions for their expressivity and performance benefits. In particular, the circles' movement is constrained within ranges relative to the screen dimensions for the X and Y axes, and relative to the predefined min and max depth values for the Z-axis. (As a reminder, these values were set in the Animation setup section.) In the case of the X and Y axes, there's an arbitrary fudge factor (notice the division by 2.75) to reduce how spread out the elements animate. This value is simply a creative decision; tweak it to suit your aesthetic preference.

Finally, the options object specifies that this entire animation should occur over a duration of 6000ms.

REVERSE COMMAND

After the primary Velocity animation call, the chain continues with a call to Velocity's reverse command. Reverse does exactly what it sounds like it: it animates the target elements back to their initial values prior to the previous Velocity call taking place. In this unique case, since start values have been force-fed into the previous Velocity call, those are the start values that reverse will animate back toward.

One of my reasons for including the reverse command in this demo is to extend the demo's overall animation duration with a single line of maintainable and expressive code. (While you could double the duration of the animation from 6000ms to 12000ms, this would result in slowing down the movement of the circles.) The convenience of the reverse command is avoiding having to respecify—by hand—all of the animation start values. It would have been a huge mess to accomplish this manually since you would have had to first store all of the randomly generated start values into memory so you could animate back to them. Hence, reverse is yet another great Velocity feature that allows the demo to accomplish a lot with just a few lines of code.

Velocity's reverse command defaults to the options object used in the previous Velocity call—including its duration, easing, and so on. In this case, since the previous call used a duration of 6000ms, so will the reverse call. The reverse command also lets you specify a new options object to extend onto the previous one. This demo uses a new easing type of easeOutQuad for added motion design flair in the animation's reverse direction.

> **TIP:** To preview the behavior of the popular easing types, visit http://easings.net.

When the reverse animation completes, a final Velocity call fades the elements out of view by transitioning their opacity values to 0 over a duration of 2000ms. This completes the demo by leaving the browser's canvas in the same visual state it began in: clean and empty! Your work here is done.

WRAPPING UP

From force-feeding, to value functions, to reverse, this walkthrough has illustrated the power of the Velocity animation engine. Hopefully, this chapter has convinced you that this book's focus on Velocity was worthwhile. In fewer than 75 lines of terse, legible, and performant code, you've created a rich 3D scene unlike anything you've seen before in pure HTML.

Let this demo serve as a concrete example of just how simple intricate-looking animations can actually be—especially when you use the right tools and employ best practices. My hope is that this book has distilled the beautiful animation work you've seen across the web into a set of tenets that are easy to grasp and follow in pursuit of your own motion design.

Now, go and design some beautiful websites and apps! Once you've put together something cool, show me on Twitter: twitter.com/shapiro.

continue learning. follow @shapiro.

INDEX

Symbols and Numbers

`$.animate()` 13

3D

    CSS primer on 156

    transforms 96

A

Adobe After Effect, animating text
    and 80

Adobe Photoshop, SVG and 104

Alerts, leveraging user response 42–43

Android

    purchasing older devices from
      eBay 144

    realities of web performance 118

Animation demo

    behaviors 148–149

    code section for animation
      setup 153–154

    code section for circle
      animation 160–164

    code section for circle creation
      154–155

    code section for container
      animation 156–159

    code structure 150–152

    overview of 147

    review 165

Animation libraries

    bypassing jQuery 6

    page scrolling functions 7

SVG support 108

types of 14

Animation reversal, performance features of
    JavaScript 7–8

Animations. *See also* Motion design

    breaking into steps 48–49

    effects on neighboring elements 130

    limiting in motion design 45

    mirroring 44

    older browsers problem 139

    older browsers solutions 139–140

    optimized coding approach to organizing
      sequenced animations 66–68

    performance. *See* Performance

    reducing concurrency 43

    reducing variety 44

    staggering 49

    standard coding approach to
      organizing sequenced
      animations 65–66

    of text. *See* Text animation

    workflows. *See* Workflows

Animations, with SVG

    animated logo example 112–113

    overview of 109

    passing properties 109

    positional attributes vs.
      transforms 110–111

    presentational attributes 110

Arguments, Velocity 16–18

Attributes, SVG markup 105–106